How to Live a Holy Life

C. E. Orr

How to Live a Holy Life

C. E. Orr

© 1st World Library – Literary Society, 2004
PO Box 2211
Fairfield, IA 52556
www.1stworldlibrary.org
First Edition

LCCN: 2004195285

Softcover ISBN: 1-4218-0112-4
Hardcover ISBN: 1-4218-0012-8
eBook ISBN: 1-4218-0212-0

Purchase *"How to Live a Holy Life"*
as a traditional bound book at:
www.1stWorldLibrary.org/purchase.asp?ISBN=1-4218-0112-4

1st World Library Literary Society is a nonprofit organization dedicated to promoting literacy by:

- Creating a free internet library accessible from any computer worldwide.
- Hosting writing competitions and offering book publishing scholarships.

Readers interested in supporting literacy through sponsorship, donations or membership please contact:
literacy@1stworldlibrary.org
Check us out at: www.1stworldlibrary.ORG
and start downloading free ebooks today.

How to Live a Holy Life
contributed by Tim, Ed & Rodney
in support of
1st World Library Literary Society

CONTENTS.

Devotional Reading 9

Preface 11

Introduction 12

The Way the Sail is Set (Poem) 16

The Model Life 18

How to Live the Christ-Life 22

The Bible Way 25

The Heavenly Way 28

Keeping the Commandments 30

Be Doers of the Word 35

Who are the Wise? 37

Keeping the Commandments a Test of Love 39

The Blessedness of Obeying God's Word 41

The Relationship We Have with Christ through Obedience 43

Our Life is to Adorn the Gospel 44

The Christian an Epistle of Christ	46
How We may Live as the Bible Reads	48
How to Keep the Word of God in the Heart	50
Man the Vehicle for Exhibiting God's Perfections	52
Some Use to Jesus (Poem)	59
Godly Living	61
Something to Do	64
Spiritual Dryness	70
Prayer	74
Keep the Roots Watered	77
Under the Fig-Tree	79
Shut the Door	82
Alone with God	84
Prayerful Remembrance (Poem)	86
He Careth for Thee	88
Consider the Lilies	93
Sorrowful Yet always Rejoicing	96
Gentleness	103

Tenderness 107

The Christian Walk 113

The Christian is to Walk Circumspectly 114

The Christian's Walk a Walk with God 118

The Latest Improved 119

Lukewarmness 134

Steadfastness 139

How to Understand God's Will 143

A View of Jesus 146

Devotion to God 148

The Golden Rule of Life 155

Timeliness in Doing Good 157

The Warfare of a Christian Life 161

Live by Faith 163

A Valuable Legacy 165

Some Scriptures for Daily Practise 167

DEVOTIONAL READING.

A person may almost be known by the books he reads. If he habitually reads bad books, we can pretty safely conclude that he is a bad man; on the other hand, if he habitually reads religious books, we can reasonably presume that he is a religious man. Why is this? It is because the nature of a person's books is usually the nature of his thoughts; and as a man thinks, so he is.

Consequently, our reading devotional literature is a great aid to our being devotional. Too few, I fear, realize how important to our spiritual advancement is the cultivation of a taste for devotional reading. As a rule, those who have a taste for spiritual books and gratify that taste prosper in the Lord, while those who have no relish for such books labor at a great disadvantage. Some one has said that "he who begins a devout life without a taste for spiritual reading may consider the ordinary difficulties multiplied in his case by ten." The most spiritual men of all ages have had a strong love for reading spiritual books. If, however, my reader happens not to have such a taste or such a love, he should not be discouraged, for it can be created and increased through perseverance in reading devotional literature. Just as a person who does not relish a certain food may learn to like it if he will persist in eating it, so a person who does not have a taste for devotional books may come to enjoy them if he will diligently and prayerfully peruse them.

Spiritual reading invigorates the intellect, warms the affections, and begets in us a desire for more of God's fulness and for a more heavenly life. It is especially helpful to prayer. When the mind is dull and the spirits low and we have no inspiration for prayer, the reading of a spiritual poem will often so stimulate the mind, raise the spirits, and animate the soul, as to make it easy for us to pray.

As to what books to read, the Bible, of course, is the best of all. But we need others. Although no other book can take the place of the Bible and none of us should neglect reading it, there are many books that can profitably be read in connection with it.

But whatever devotional book you are reading, do not read too fast. Think and digest as you go. Let there be a frequent lifting of the heart to God in prayer. It is not the bee that flies so swiftly from flower to flower that gathers the honey, but the bee that goes down into the flower. A few sentences taken into the mind and heart, and dwelt upon until they have become a part of us, are better than many pages read superficially.

PREFACE.

If the reading of this little book encourages any on their pilgrim way; if it arouses them to greater diligence; if it creates in them a stronger desire to live more like Christ; if it gives them a better understanding of how to live, - this poor servant of the Lord will be fully rewarded for all his labor.

Even among the children of God in this beautiful gospel light of the evening there is an inclination, on the part of a few at least, and maybe more than a few, to slow down and not be their very best and most active for God. We hope that this little book will arouse such ones to greater zeal and earnestness. Diligence, yea, constant application, is the secret of success in all manner of life and especially in the Christian life.

This volume is written for all those who desire to please God with a well-spent life. It is sent forth in Jesus' name, with a prayer - that God bless and help both the reader and the writer to live life at its very best and fulfil the purpose of God concerning them.

Your humble servant in Christian love,

The Author.

INTRODUCTION.

We have only one life to live, only one. Think of this for a moment. Here we are in this world of time making the journey of life. Each day we are farther from the cradle and nearer the grave. Solemn thought. See the mighty concourse of human lives; hear their heavy tread in their onward march. Some are just beginning life's journey; some are midway up the hill, some have reached the top, and some are midway down the western slope. But where are we all going? Listen, and you will hear but one answer - "Eternity." Beyond the fading, dying gleams of the sunset of life lies a boundless, endless ocean called Eternity. Thitherward you and I are daily traveling.

Time is like a great wheel going its round. On and on it goes. Some are stepping on and some are stepping off. But where are these latter stepping? Into eternity. See that old man with bent form, snow-white locks, and tottering steps. His has been a long round, but he has made it at last. See the middle-aged. His round has not been so long, but he must step off. See the youth. He has been on only a little while, but he is brought to the stepping-off place. He thought his round would be much longer. He supposed he was fairly getting started when that icy hand was laid upon him and the usher said, "Come, you have made your round, and you must go." The infant that gave its first faint cry this morning may utter its last feeble wail tonight. And thus they go. But where? Eternity.

If you were to start today and ask each person you met the question, "Where are you going?" and, if possible, you were to travel the world over and ask each one of earth's inhabitants, there could be but one answer - "Eternity."

> "Oh, eternity,
> Long eternity!
> Hear the solemn footsteps
> Of eternity."

Only one life to live! Only one life, and then we must face vast, endless eternity. We shall pass along the pathway of life but once. Every step we take is a step that can never be taken again. With this fact in mind, who does not feel like calling upon the All-wise to direct his every step. If when we make a misstep we could go back and step it over, then there would not be such great necessity to step carefully. But we can never go back. We are leaving footprints. Just as our steps are, so will the footprints be which will tell the story of our life. If we had a score of lives to live, how to live this one would not be of such great moment. We should then have nineteen lives in which to correct the errors and sins of this one; but alas! we have but one. What, then, should we seek more earnestly than to know *how to live?*

We doubt not but there is in the heart of the reader a strong desire to live life as it should be lived. Thank God, you can. You desire your life to be like the fertile oasis, where the weary traveler refreshes himself. You have seen the rays of light lingering upon the hillside and treetop and gilding the fleecy cloud after the sun had gone down. You desire the beautiful rays of light from your life to linger long after your sun has gone down. You can have it that way. The deeds you do will live after you are gone. They are the footprints. Some one has said that we each day are here building the house we are going to occupy in eternity. If this be true, nothing should concern us so much as how to live. Some men are devoting their time and the power of their intellects to invention; some are studying statesmanship; some are studying the arts, others the sciences; but we have come to learn a little more about how to live. Many are thinking much about how they wish to die, but let us learn how to live. If we live well, we shall die well.

Since we have but one life to live and with it we must face eternity, I am sure there are many who want to make the most of life. There are many who want to be their best in life. This is not a play-ground, or a place to trifle with time. It is a place of work and effort, a place of purpose and earnestness, a place to do something. Life is not given us to squander nor fritter away, but was given us to accomplish a purpose in the mind of the Creator. If we will set ourselves to live as we should, God will help us and no man can hinder us. We are purchasing treasures for eternity by making a proper use of time. To trifle away time is indeed to be the greatest of spendthrifts. If you squander a dollar, you may regain it; but a moment wasted can never be regained.

There is great responsibility in life. It means much to live. The time was when you and I were not, now we are. We are, and there can never come a time when we shall not be. You and I shall always exist somehow, somewhere. One sweet thought to me is that I have time enough to do all that God intends for me to do, and do it well. Then comes another thought - a thought that awes: the good that I do, the sum of my usefulness, will be less than it should be if I spend a moment of time uselessly. God will give us all the time we need to accomplish all he purposes us to accomplish, but he does not give us one moment to trifle away.

The mission of this little volume is to strengthen and energize and help you to spend life as you should. May it please the Great Teacher, who has promised to "show us the path of life," to bless this little work and by it help some one to a pure and noble life and to the accomplishment of all God's design in giving them life.

The Author.

THE WAY THE SAIL IS SET.

I stood beside the open sea;
 The ships went sailing by;
The wind blew softly o'er the lea;
 The sun had cloudless sky.

Some ships sailed eastward, some sailed west,
 Some north, some southward trend.
How can ships sail this way and that?
 But one way blows the wind.

An old sea-captain made reply
 (His locks with salt-spray wet):
"'Tis not the wind decides the course;
 'Tis way the sails are set."

*   *   *   *   *

I stand beside the sea of life;
 The ships go sailing by;
The winds blow fair from heaven's land;
 No clouds bedim the sky.

But one sails eastward, one sails west,
 One north, one southward goes:
How can ships sail this way and that
 With selfsame wind that blows?

C. E. Orr

A voice made answer to my soul:
 "'Tis not how blows the gale;
Each voyager decides the goal
 By way he sets the sail." - Selected.

THE MODEL LIFE.

In doing anything, it is always well to have a model by which to fashion our work. In fact, nothing is done without a pattern, either real or imaginary. The little boy making a toy has in in his mind a model by which he is framing his work. Likewise, the sculptor has in his mind a model, and as the "marble wastes, the image grows" into the likeness of the vision in his soul.

To live this one life of ours as it should be lived, we must have a perfect model after which to pattern. Thank God, this perfect model of life can be found. Of all the vast number of lives that have been lived since Adam down to this present day, there has been only one that we can take as a model. This one is the life of Jesus. He says, "I am the life." To live this life of ours well, to live it to the highest degree of perfection, we must fashion it according to the glorious life of Christ. The life of Jesus is the model life for every other human life. He invites us, yea, commands us, to follow him, to step in his steps, to walk as he walked.

There have been many good men in the world, but none of them afford us a true pattern of life. There was a man who said, "Be ye followers of me," but he immediately added, "even as I also am of Christ." Man may so live as to reveal to us the life of Christ. We can then follow, not them, but the Christ-life they manifested through them.

Let me here say a word on a subject on which we may have more to say hereafter. The grandest, noblest work man has ever done is by his life to reveal the life of Christ to another, thereby helping that person to be fashioned more after the image of Jesus. A little flower grew in a place so shaded that no ray from the sun could fall directly upon it. A window was so situated that at a certain time in the afternoon it refracted the sun's rays and threw them upon the flower, thus giving it color and beauty, and aiding it to bloom. Some people are living in the dense shade. No light from Christ has ever shined upon them. If you so live as to refract the life of Christ and turn it upon them and thus stamp upon them a holier life, you have not lived in vain. To set the life of Christ in its purity and beauty before some one and influence him, though only a little, to live better and love Jesus more, is a work the worth of which can never be computed. He who helps another to a better way of living does more than he who gains great worldly honor and riches. Blessed indeed is that life which causes some other life to be more like Christ. Oh, may this thought seize upon our hearts and fill us with a greater passion to live the life of God.

We are told by the voice of Scripture to be "followers of God as dear children." When children are dear to the heart of the parent, he loves to have them obey him. God's children are dear to him, and he would have them follow him. To follow God is to imitate him, or be like him. This is the true way of life.

A text of Scripture as rendered by the Revised Version is very appropriate here: "Like as he which has called you is holy, be ye yourselves also holy in all manner of living." 1 Pet. 1:15. Only those who live godly in their entire manner of life are spending the days of their pilgrimage as they should. Jesus has walked the true way of life; we are told to walk in his steps. If we will step each day just where Jesus stepped, then on looking back, we can not see a footprint of our own; but if we take a single misstep, our footprint will show our departure from the true way of life. How deep and awful are the words of Scripture wherein we are commanded to walk even as "Jesus walked"! Jesus says, "I am the way." There is no other right and perfect way. If we will walk as Jesus walked, then we shall walk in the true path of life. This only is the pathway that leads up to the golden gates of glory and the sweet fields of heaven. That bright world of bliss encourages us on. If we will follow Jesus and live as he lived, God's approval will be upon us, and his outstretched hand will help us along life's way and finally over the turbulent river of death to the sunlit shore of eternal rest.

Many times we may become wearied and think the toils of the way almost too heavy; but when we remember that it is the way that Jesus trod, then the heavens open to our view, we look forward to the mansion prepared for us, and the toils of the way grow lighter.

See that aged pilgrim journeying down the western slope of life. The sun is nearing the setting. Long and toilsome has been his pilgrimage, but he has walked in the path his Savior trod. For many years his life has been hid with Christ in God. In Him he has lived and moved and had his being. Now he is making his last step on the shore of time; he passes out of our sight through the gates into that land where toils are ended and the sun never sets. But his life was the life of Jesus. He was holy as God is holy; he walked as Jesus walked. This is how to live. This is the true way of life and the only way to life eternal. He who does not live with Christ on earth can not live with him in heaven, and he who does not live as Jesus lived does not live as he should. The life of Christ was the perfect life. Ours is perfect to the degree that we imitate him.

Take my life, O Christ divine,
Make it holy, just like thine;
Every act and thought and word
Be an outflow from my God.

Guide my feet and keep my heart;
Let me not from thee depart;
Let me breathe thy warming love,
That my soul be drawn above.

Draw me, Jesus, closer draw;
Thy strong arm around me throw;
Draw me to thy pierced side;
In thy bosom let me hide.

Teach me all thy will and word,
That my life be filled with God;
Teach me, Lamb of Calvary,
How to live this life for thee.

HOW TO LIVE THE CHRIST-LIFE.

Man can not naturally live the Christ-life. But Christ has promised to come into our hearts and live in us. In order that we may have Christ dwell in our hearts and that we may live his life, there must be a giving up of our self-life. There must be annihilation of self that Christ may live. It is truly wonderful and as glorious as it is wonderful that man can live the life of Christ in this world. But here is the secret: it is man ceasing to live the self-life and Christ living in him.

Imagine a hollow brass figure in the exact image of a man. Suppose you fill this hollow figure with a kind of life which we shall call self-life. This life goes to using the hands and feet, and eyes, ears, tongue, in short, all the members of this brass figure, but using them in the interest of itself. Now you desire to make a change; you want that image to speak, act, and think only for you. You must first put to death the life that is using the figure, cleanse it entirely out, and then get into it yourself. Once in, you can use all the members of that image for yourself. Your body is that image. There was a life in you that used all the members of your body in the interest of self. But there has been a change. You were made a new creature. The life you once had was put to death - was crucified; then Christ stepped into your heart, and now he uses all the members of your body for himself. You still live, yet not you, but Christ lives in you. Once you did things for yourself; now you do them for Christ. Just as you once lived purposely and intentionally for yourself, now you do things purposely and intentionally for Jesus, because it is he that lives, and not you yourself. You remember how once you would plan for yourself. In the evening as you lay upon your bed and again in the morning and throughout the day you would think about what you were going to eat or drink, what you were going to have for clothing, where you were going to live, where you were going to go, and what you were going to do. But now you are changed; you are a new creature. Now it is not you that lives, but Christ lives in you. Now you eat not for yourself but for Jesus. You now go, not where self would lead you, but where that life in you loves to go and would have you go. You do things, not for yourself, but for Jesus.

O Christ, I die, that thou mayst live,
  That thou mayst live in me;
That all I think or speak or do,
  May be, O Lord, for thee.

May not the least of self remain,
  But all be put to death.
Oh, may I nothing do for self,
  Nor draw one selfish breath!

To have my Savior live in me,
  To occupy the whole,
To make my heart his royal throne
  And take complete control -

'Tis all I ask; 'tis all I wish;
  'Tis all my heart's desire,
Content if but a wayside bush

To hold God's holy fire.

Low at thy feet, O Christ, I fall
 A yielded lump of clay,
For thee to mold me as thou wilt,
 To have thy own sweet way.

THE BIBLE WAY.

If the Bible had not been given us, we should not always know the way that Jesus walked. But he has given us his Word. The way of the Bible is the way of Christ, and is therefore the true path of life. O pilgrim to the heavenly kingdom, the Word of God will be a lamp unto thy feet and a light unto thy way. It will lighten you home. There will never be a day so dark but the beams of light from the blessed Bible will pierce through the darkness and fall with a bright radiance upon your pathway. If sometimes you can not see just where Jesus stepped, take the precious Book of God, and it will be a lamp to show you the way he trod. One wintry morning a father went a long distance through the deep snow to feed his sheep. A few hours later a little boy was sent to call his father home. The child was carefully stepping in the footprints before him, but soon a dark cloud arose and the blinding snow-storm so dimmed his eye that he frequently stepped aside. In the beautiful, clear light of the Bible we can see all the way that Jesus trod. If we will walk according to the Bible, we shall walk as Jesus walked and not show a double track. Make the blessed Word of God your guide if you would walk aright the path of life and be happy.

"And often for your comfort you will read the Guide and Chart:

It has wisdom for the mind and sweet solace for the heart;
It will serve you as a mentor; it will guide you sure and straight
All the time that you will journey, be the ending soon or late."

'The Scriptures are given by inspiration of God and are profitable for doctrine, for reproof, for correction, for instruction in righteousness, that the man of God may be perfect' 2 Tim. 3:16. If by faith we receive into our hearts the instruction in righteousness as given by the Scriptures, it will make us perfect in this life. O reader, if you would know how to live, study the Bible. It points out the way clearly and plainly. Let its truths in all their power reach to the depth of thy heart. Let thy soul seize upon the Bible and drink its strength and sweetness as the bee sips the sweetness from the flower. As the animal eats the plant and by assimilation converts it into animal life, so eat the Book of God and convert it into human life. It is the food of angels. But rather than its being the Bible converted into human life, it is human life transformed into the purity of the Bible. There are great depths to the Bible. The simplest text contains depths to which we can ever be descending.

They who would live a perfect life must set the life of Christ before them as portrayed by the Holy Scriptures. You can not see much of this perfect life by a passing glance. It is he who looks into the perfect law of liberty and continues to look that will see the perfect life which it pictures. The artist must look long at the landscape and get it imaged upon his soul before he can produce it upon the canvas. The Bible description of the life of Christ must fill your soul with admiration and with a strong desire to possess it. Your heart must lay hold upon it until that life is focused and printed upon your own soul. It is like the art of photographing. The object must be set before the heart.

The Bible is the light that shines the image of Christ upon the soul. For the pure in heart to develop into higher spiritual life, they must gain such an admiration for the beauty of Christ that they will long to possess him in greater fulness. The pleading of the heart will be, "Lord, let thy beauty be upon us." Their souls will follow hard after his perfections. In no other way will the soul unfold and develop into the higher Christian life. He who has not learned how to grow in grace has not yet learned how to live. To live life in the best possible manner is to be making constant progress. Oh, let us give this world our best life! When we are nearing the end of the way and life's sun is sinking low, if on looking back we can see nothing but a life spent in the service of God, walking in the light of his Word, this will afford us untold satisfaction.

>O blessed Word of eternal life,
>The lamp to guide the way
>Through this weary world of sin and strife
>To heaven's perfect day!

THE HEAVENLY WAY.

There is a heaven. There is a place of rest and happiness. I have not gone to heaven, but heaven has come to me; therefore I know there is a heaven. Many who have eaten oranges have never been in a land where oranges grow, but these persons know there must be such a land, because they have tasted its fruit. Likewise, I know there is a heaven because I daily taste its joy.

Not only is there a heaven, but there is a way to heaven. All can go who will. Heaven is a holy place, and the way to heaven is a holy way. A prophet of God said, "An highway shall be there, and a way, and it shall be called the way of holiness." The Christian dwells in a heavenly place.

The writer to the saints at Ephesus says, "He hath raised us up together, and made us sit together in heavenly places." To live in a heavenly place, we must live a heavenly life. Those who do not live a heavenly life on earth will never live in heaven. The heavenly life is the only life worth living. It is the only life that ends in heaven. The way of holiness is the way of happiness. Holy and happy is the true and right life of man. This one brief life of ours should be constant holiness and happiness. Without these, life is not as it should be. It is our privilege in Christ to walk the path of life in perfect peace and joy and in perfect holiness. Such a life will flow out into an eternity of joys unspeakable.

Wait thou on God, O soul of mine!
 Listen to know his will;
Light will come from the golden throne
 If thou, O soul, be still.

If thou wouldst sail on tranquil sea,
 Wait thou on God, my soul.
Speak, act, and think alone in him;
 Sweet rest shall be thy goal.

If thou wouldst have life's way to be
 Verdant as the growing sod,
Take each step 'neath the guiding eye,
 Keep in close touch with God.

Sweet heavenly life! sweet happy life!
 Thy joys increase each day.
O soul of mine, press up and on
 This high and holy way.

KEEPING THE COMMANDMENTS.

God's Word is pure. Heaven itself and the great white throne is no more pure than the Word of God. That life may be pure, it must be in sweet harmony with the blessed Bible. A life that is lived in obedience to the Bible is as pure as the Bible. Such a life is pure enough for heaven. The writer of Revelation, being in the Spirit, saw "a pure river of water of life, clear as crystal, proceeding out of the throne of God and of the Lamb." This pure stream was the wonderful word of life. It was as pure as its source, which was the throne of God. The life through which this pure stream flows will be as pure as the throne.

One of the Psalm-writers said, "The words of the Lord are pure words: as silver tried in a furnace of earth, purified seven times." "Thy word is pure; therefore thy servant loveth it." The writer of Proverbs says, "Every word of God is pure." When the veil is drawn aside and our souls are brought face to face with the purity of the Bible, then we understand that a Bible life is the best, purest, noblest, and holiest life that can be lived upon the earth.

  O soul of mine, unveil thine eye,
   Look upward to thy God,
   A wreath of purity to see
   Crowning his every word.

In the following words we have the sum of all true and right living: "Let us hear the conclusion of the whole matter: fear God and keep his commandments; for this is the whole duty of man." Eccl. 12:13. This text as rendered in the Septuagint version brings out clearer the true signification: "Hear the end of the matter, the sum. Fear God and keep his commandments: for this is the whole man." Man is not entire, he is not complete as originally intended, when not keeping all the commands of God. Something is lacking in the life that is not in full obedience to every word of God.

The Bible speaks of a beautiful city in that bright, celestial world. It is a city of pure gold, clear as glass. Its walls are of jasper; its twelve foundations are garnished with all manner of precious stones; its twelve gates are gates of pearl; its streets are pure gold. In that fair city there is no sin, no pain, no sickness; sorrow and trouble never come there; a tear shall never fall from any eye, for no tears are there. There is no death in that wonderful city so fair. In the midst of the street stands the tree of life. Oh, who does not desire to dwell forever and forever in that city of love and light when the pains and sorrows, the trials and tears, of this weary life are over?

Listen while I read to you in accents clear, distinct, and unmistakable - "Blessed are they that do his commandments, that they may have right to the tree of life, and may enter in through the gates into the city." Rev. 22:14. O traveler to eternity, your entrance into the beautiful, glorious city of God depends upon your conduct respecting the commandments of God while you are making the journey across the turbulent sea of life. Keeping the commandments of God is man's whole duty. If he does his whole duty through life, he will come up out of the dark valley and shadow of death, and find the gates of pearl unfolding. Who will not cleave to the commandments of God? Who will not obey his voice and walk daily in his holy ways? The obedient will be rewarded by an unfading inheritance in that eternal city of gold. There is a beautiful mansion in the great house of God for every obedient soul. Oh, how blessed!

> I am thinking of heaven tonight,
> Of the mansion prepared there for me,
> Where Jesus my Savior now dwells,
> And where I am longing to be.

Will not heaven be well worth a life of obedience to the Word of God, though obedience calls us through storms of persecutions, furnaces of trials, oceans of tribulations, and years of toil and suffering? To Moses the reproaches of Christ were greater treasures than the riches of Egypt, "for he had respect unto the recompense of the reward." Sit quiet for a moment and by a strong eye of faith look away into heaven and see that bright mansion prepared for you. See those jasper walls, those pearly gates, and those golden walks. See the crown of life, the harp of God, and the light of the Lamb. Shall we not bear the trials of life a little longer in patience? Shall we not be watchful to walk in God's ways and obey him, that this rich inheritance may be ours forever? Methinks I can hear a reply coming from the depths of many a sincere, trusting heart - "Yes, I will live in humble obedience to God on earth, that I may be with him forever in that celestial city of light." God bless you!

Beyond the shores of time and the kingdoms of this

world is a kingdom called the kingdom of heaven. It is the place where God has his great white throne, around which the angels play upon their golden harps and shout, "Blessing and honor and glory and praise and might be unto God forever and ever." It is around this throne that those who have passed through the tribulations and the trying scenes of this lower world and burst through the gates of death are singing redemption's sweet song. Who does not desire to join that happy, heavenly throng and wave those palms and wear those white robes and sing those sweet songs over beyond the shadowy vale of death? I seem to hear many voices saying, "I hope to be among that blood-washed throng." Let me tell you in all tenderness and love, but very plainly, that the realization of your hope depends entirely upon how you live while here in this world. Oh, how much in that great and awful future is depending upon our manner of life in this time-world! Let us learn to live well, to be our best every day.

We may dream of a home in heaven; we may entertain hopes of seeing Jesus and of inheriting a mansion on the shores of eternal bliss; we may imagine ourselves walking through the blooming fields of paradise and sitting beneath the tree of life; but our dreams, our hopes, and our imaginations will never be realized unless we carefully keep the commandments of God. More than a profession is necessary; obedience is the only door into the kingdom of God. Jesus said, "Not every one that sayeth unto me, Lord, Lord, shall enter the kingdom of heaven; but he that doeth the will of my Father which is in heaven." Until our faith pierces through and beholds the beauties and the realities of God so we can say from the very depths of the soul, "I delight to do thy will, O God." and, "My meat and my drink is to do the will of Him that sent me," we have not fully entered the true and right pathway of life. Keeping the commands of God is the whole man and the whole of a perfect life.

BE DOERS OF THE WORD.

I want to remind you again that the mission of this little volume is to teach you how to live. The life beyond depends on the life here. Let me emphasize what I have repeatedly said before: to live as we should, we must live by every word of God. To live by every word of God is not only to hear it but also to do it. We have learned that, in order to enter the city of God and eat of the tree of life, we must *do* his commandments, and also that it is not "every one that sayeth, Lord, Lord, that shall enter the kingdom of heaven, but he that doeth the will of my Father which is in heaven."

Now I will read you a text from the Epistle of James, "But be ye doers of the word, and not hearers only, deceiving your own selves." We are living in a careless age. The Word of God is being treated with neglect. Many are hearing it, but alas! how few are doing it! In this way people deceive themselves. They think they are on their way to heaven, when they are not. The only way to heaven is by doing the commandments. To illustrate this, I will refer you to a few texts. "If thine enemy hunger, feed him." Rom. 12:20. "Whosoever shall smite thee on thy right cheek, turn to him the other also." Matt. 5:39. "And as ye would that men should do to you, do ye also to them likewise." Luke 6:31. If it comes most natural for us to live according to these texts, we can begin to conclude that our hearts are right with God. However, we must have a heart that does not rebel against any text in the Bible.

We are exhorted earnestly by the apostle Peter to make our "calling and election sure." The only way to do so is to live to every word of God. Oh, my dear reader, those sweet hopes you have had of reaching heaven and of seeing Jesus and those dear loved ones who have gone before you to that other side will never be realized by you unless you be a diligent doer of the Word of God. I feel like warning you against all carelessness and neglect, and to keep yourself in the love of God. See that your heart and life reads each day as the Bible reads, and you will then have an unshaken foundation for your faith and hope. If you would know how to live and make the best of life, read the Bible much and conform your life to its teaching.

WHO ARE THE WISE?

Who is a foolish man? It is a man who hears the sayings of Jesus and fails to do them. He is likened to a man who was foolish enough to build his house upon the sand. This man would better not have built at all, for the cost of building was lost. He could have had the money for his use and enjoyment if he had not wasted it in building a house on the sand. A foolish man, indeed! Who is a wise man? It is the man who hears the sayings of Jesus and does them. He is likened to a man who built his house upon a rock. From a temporal standpoint nothing else is so conducive to man's happiness as a good home. No better use can be made of money than to spend it in the building of a home, provided the house be built upon a sure foundation. A man who hears God's Word and does it is likened to such a man. To build up a Christian character in obedience to the Bible is the greatest wisdom. That is building a mansion in heaven.

A real, true Christian experience and life cost something, but they pay, because they will stand. A mere profession of Christianity may cost something also, but it does not pay, since it will not stand. A man who erects his house upon the sand can build at less cost than he who digs deep and lays his foundation upon the rock, but at the very time when the former man most needs his house - when the winds blow and the rain falls - that is when it is destroyed. On the other hand, the man who builds upon a rock has a house to shelter him through the storms. Likewise, he who builds up a Christian experience in obedience to the Word of God will have something to serve him in a time of need.

We thus learn from Jesus' parable of the wise and the foolish house-builders that obeying the Bible is the true way of life.

KEEPING THE COMMANDMENTS
A TEST OF LOVE.

We are commanded to love God. It is the first and greatest commandment. Love is more than an emotion; it is an act of the will. A mother loves her child constantly, though she may not always experience the emotions of love. Her care for her child is a proof of her love. We may not always experience a feeling of love toward God, but we can always love him. Our love is measured, not by our emotions, but by our obedience - our service. We labor for those we love, and the love makes the labor light. It is not an irksome thing to obey God when we love him.

It is possible to make a profession of love to God and not really love him. It may be that many are deceived at this point. One scripture says, "If any man love God, the same is known of him." Jesus says, "Why call ye me Lord, Lord, and do not the things which I say?" Love is something more than mere words. It is useless to make a profession of love to Jesus and not do what he says. A husband can not convince his wife of his love by a mere profession of love, but he can convince her by his acts. We are to love, not in word and tongue only, but also in deed and in truth. Again, Jesus says, "If a man love me, he will keep my words." Here is an unfailing test of love. If you will not obey God, he knows you do not love him, no matter how much you may profess to love him.

So again we are reminded by the Holy Bible that, in order to spend this brief life of ours as we should, we must keep the commandments of God. No other life will find acceptance with God. No other life will please him. He desires your love most certainly, but he wants such love as will prompt you to obey him. Do not measure your Christian experience by your feelings, but measure it by your obedience as proceeding from an internal principle. When you find something in your heart that causes you to obey God no matter how you feel, you have good reason to hope that you are a Christian.

In subsequent chapters I will tell you something of what God's Word teaches, but, first of all, I desire to fully convince you, and to help you to feel, that the right and true way of life is in obedience to its teaching.

THE BLESSEDNESS OF OBEYING GOD'S WORD.

Everything is said in the Scriptures that can be said to show us the need of living in harmony with the Bible. If our lives are out of harmony with one text in that blessed book, we are not yet fitted for heaven. We can never be admitted into the everlasting kingdom of God if we knowingly refuse or neglect to live to every word of God. We are therefore exhorted, beseeched, entreated, encouraged, warned, and commanded to obey every text in the Bible. We are encouraged to obedience by being told of the blessedness of keeping the commandments.

It is natural for mothers to love to have their children well spoken of. We do not fault them for this. When a young man, by his good deportment, is gaining a fair name, mothers, when together, will remark, "It is blessed to be the mother of a young man like that." There was a woman who heard of the fame of a young man. He was casting out devils, healing the sick, opening blinded eyes, and unstopping deaf ears, and consequently he was gaining a wide and favorable reputation. This woman came to the young man and with that mother in her heart said to him, "Blessed is the womb that bear thee, and the paps which thou hast sucked." It was, indeed, blessed to be the mother of this young man. An angel from heaven acknowledged this. In speaking to Mary of the birth of Jesus (for he was the young man), the angel said, "Hail, thou that are highly favored, the Lord is with thee: blessed art thou among women." She was more highly favored than any other woman on earth, because she was to become the mother of the Son of God. Can it be that any one can be more blessed than this happy mother of Jesus? Let us hear his reply to the woman - "But he said, Yea, rather blessed are they that hear the word of God and keep it." Jesus did not deny that it was blessed to be his mother, but said that those who hear God's word and keep it are rather, or more, blessed. God favors those who obey him. "The willing and obedient shall eat the good of the land." "Hadst thou hearkened unto my commandments, then wouldst thy peace be like a river." Happiness is the result of obedience, and heaven is the final reward.

THE RELATIONSHIP WE HAVE WITH CHRIST THROUGH OBEDIENCE.

The reason why it is more blessed to obey the Word of God than to be the mother of Jesus is obvious. Spiritual things are higher than physical things. Spiritual relation is closer than natural relation. Brotherhood in Christ is closer than brotherhood in the flesh. A brother in the Spirit is dearer to us than a son of our own mother. Obedience to God makes us one with God. Mary was the mother of Jesus after the flesh, but God's children enjoy such a relation after the spirit. At one time somebody brought word to Jesus that his mother and his brethren stood outside desiring to see him. "But he answered and said unto him that told him, Who is my mother? and who are my brethren? And he stretched forth his hand toward his disciples, and said, Behold my mother and my brethren! for whoever shall do the will of my Father which is in heaven, the same is my brother, and sister, and mother." Matt. 12:48-50. Every one who desires to spend life in the highest possible degree of perfection should make a constant study of the Bible and should carefully and diligently obey all its precepts. Doing this will bring him into the closest possible relationship with God and will make life the best man can live.

OUR LIFE IS TO ADORN THE GOSPEL.

To adorn is to make attractive, to beautify. We are exhorted by the apostle Paul to adorn the doctrine of the New Testament by our every-day life. This thought should be a powerful incentive to close living with God and assiduously keeping all of his commandments. Who would not take pleasure in adorning the teachings of Jesus by a pure life? This is the joy of the Christian's heart. He cares nothing for the adornings of the world, but oh, that he may so live as to make beautiful the blessed Bible! - this is happiness enough to him.

In another of the Pauline Epistles we are commanded to "let our manner of life be as it becometh the gospel of Christ." To become is also to make attractive or to give a better appearance to. An article of dress is becoming to us when it gives us a better appearance. We speak of any one's bad conduct as not being becoming to him. We are to become the gospel of Christ by holy living. When a life is lived as God designed that life should be, that life will be an adornment to the Scriptures.

God will beautify his children with the glories of his redeeming grace; he will adorn them with a meek and quiet spirit, which in his sight is very precious, that they, in turn, may adorn his commandments. As a bride decks herself with jewels, so the heavenly Father beautifies his children with the robe of righteousness.

The life of a Christian is God's special treasure. "They shall be mine," says the Lord, "in that day when I make up my jewels," or "special treasure" as rendered by the margin (see Mal. 3:17). By reading the context we learn that it is those who fear the Lord that are his jewels. To fear God and keep his commandments is man's whole duty. It is a perfect life. Such a life is the Lord's jewel. Such a life is recorded in heaven. Oh, how animating is such knowledge! How it strengthens our hearts to live a righteous life. To live a life that is worthy to be recorded in heaven and is a special treasure to God is truly wonderful. Our souls are awed by such a thought. Oh, how it ought to move our hearts to carefulness in life! How diligent we should be to walk as worthy citizens of our heavenly state! Some day the Lord will come and gather up these holy lives and place them in his heavenly courts above, where they shall shine as the stars forever.

> Oh, take this life, this life of mine
> (To thee, O God, 'tis freely given),
> And polish it, that it may shine,
> And ornament thy Word divine.

THE CHRISTIAN AN EPISTLE OF CHRIST.

The life we live is being read. We are not going through the world unnoticed. Some one is looking on, and some one is to some extent fashioning his life after ours. Our life each day is being written down in some one's memory. My own dear children group around me at times and talk of their mother, who has gone to heaven. Her pure and holy life written in their memory is read over and over to each other and to me. She still lives as an epistle in their hearts. They read her daily life while she was with them, and they continue to read it since she is gone. Christians are said to be the epistle of Christ (2 Cor. 3:3). To read their life is to read the life of Jesus. All the Bible that many will ever read is what they read in the lives of Christians.

Life will be read just as it is, not as it may pretend to be. It is not what we pretend to be, but what we really are, that will go down in the memory of others. Those who read our lives have a way of reading between the lines. We should strive not so much to make life holy as to be holy. If you are holy, then live just what you are. We should never strive to be what we are not. The only way whereby the Bible may be read in the life is to get it in the heart. People will never read the Word of God in your life simply because you have a neat little Testament in your pocket or a large family Bible on your center table. The Bible can get into the life only by beginning at the heart. There is power in the Word of God, but it works from within. "Let the word of Christ dwell in you richly." It will transform the life so that the life will read just like the Holy Scriptures.

The Word of God is a lamp to light us into a holy life. If we follow its instructions in righteousness, it will make us perfect. It reveals our imperfections and thus gives us an opportunity to make improvements. To discover an imperfection in the life is not a bad thing, and we need not think we are any the worse for the discovery. It is only when we let the imperfection remain after it is revealed to us, that we become worse.

The heart that comes under the influence of the Bible will bear the image of Jesus, but of this I shall have more to say elsewhere. So I conclude here by saying, live upon the Word of God, desire the sincere milk of the Word, and you will be an epistle of Christ. We should feel the responsibility that is upon us, remembering that all the Bible some will ever read is what they read in your life and mine. Oh! let us see that it reads in our life as it does in the book, lest those who follow us will not walk in the footprints of Jesus.

HOW WE MAY LIVE AS THE BIBLE READS.

It is just as natural and easy for a Christian to live the Christian life as it is for a sinner to live a sinful life. The sinner needs make no effort to live a sinful life; he lives it naturally and easily. Life proceeds from the heart. The heart is the fountain, and the life is the stream. As the fountain is, so the stream will be. It is not difficult to live a Christian life when our hearts are pure. This is the secret of purity of life.

The important question, then, is, "How can I have a pure heart?" Hearts are made pure by the blood of Jesus. Then comes the command, "Keep thyself pure." That the heart may be kept pure, it must be kept filled with that which is pure. To keep darkness out of a room, we need only to keep it filled with light. Carefully closing up every crevice will not suffice if the light goes out. Darkness will be present. But simply keep the room filled with light, and no effort is required to keep darkness out. In like manner no effort need be made to keep impurity out of the heart and keep the heart filled with that which is pure.

But what is pure? "The word of God is pure, as silver tried in a furnace of fire, purified seven times." "Thy word is very pure; therefore thy servant loveth it." "Let the word of Christ dwell in you richly," and your heart will be kept pure. The Psalm-writer said, "Thy word have I hid in my heart, that I may not sin against thee." Here is the only way to a sinless life. Keep the heart filled with the Word of God. It is the way to live as the Bible reads. To have a nicely bound volume of the Scriptures lying on the center table will not keep the life sinless. We must have the Word in our heart. One night while I was waiting for a train in one of our large Eastern cities, I went into a mission. A man arose and said he had read the Bible through forty-two times and could quote whole books of it from memory. Later in his talk he said he committed sin more or less every day. The Word of God did not keep him from sinning, for he had it in his head instead of in his heart.

To live a Bible life is the only true and right way to live, and in order to live such a life, we need to have the Word written in the heart. "I will put my laws into their mind, and write them in their hearts." Heb. 8: 10. Let us illustrate this by taking a single text: "Having food and raiment let us be therewith content." When we have these words in the heart, they will be true in the life. All fret and worry and murmurings will be banished out of the life when the heart is full of the truth.

HOW TO KEEP THE WORD OF GOD IN THE HEART.

Since keeping the Word of God in the heart is the only way to successful Christian living, you will at once want to know how to keep it in the heart. The Word is kept in the heart the same as food is kept in the body. The food is eaten, and then by the process of assimilation it becomes a part of the body. This is something of a mystery; nevertheless we all know it to be true. We feel weak in body, but soon after we partake of food, we feel stronger. Somehow that food gets into the life and makes us stronger. Now, "man shall not live by bread alone, but by every word that proceedeth out of the mouth of God." We can eat the Word of God, and we *must* eat it in order to get it into our heart and life. By eating and the process of assimilation the Word becomes a part of our inner being. We eat it by faith, and the Spirit assimilates it into our hearts.

Let us take a text: "In honor preferring one another." It is blessed to have an experience like this. To feel happy when others are honored and we are not is certainly a desirable experience. We can have it. As you read the above text, love it, admire it, desire it, ask for it, believe you receive it, - and you have it. It will be a truth of beauty and of power in your soul and life. But remember, you must have an eagerness for it. You must lay hold upon it as the infant does upon the mother's breast. The same is true with every text in the Bible. Eat the entire book, and thus you will have it as a glorious source of power and purity in your life.

MAN THE VEHICLE FOR EXHIBITING GOD'S PERFECTIONS.

Man was created for a purpose, and that purpose was to glorify his Creator (Isa. 43:7). But man sinned and came short of the glory of God. The Lord, that he may yet be glorified in the man, provides a way of redemption. Through the redemption we have in Christ we can live to the glory of God. This is God's purpose. The whole of life should be such as will glorify the Creator, and all that we do should be done with that end in view. God help us. Living for God, honoring his Word, magnifying his name - this is the duty of man. Awful responsibility! Oh, what carefulness it should work in us. What vehement desire! what earnest seeking after God! that we may live such a life.

Jesus was here in the world and was the light of the world. He had a human body and in that body lived a life that glorified God. That was an exemplary life. Such a life, and such a life only, is to the glory of God. We must fashion our life after his if we would spend life as we should. To know how Jesus lived is to know how we should live. Every life that is in the likeness of Christ's life is accepted of God. No other life can be. While Christ was here in the body, he was in the express image of the Father. The true, holy character of God was revealed through Jesus' human life to a lost and sinning world. God had done all he could to reveal his true character to man by laws, ceremonies, and ordinances; but these were only the shadow of the true life that was to be the light of the world. Christ was both God and man. Having a physical form, which is visible, he could set the holiness of God in plain view before the world. If you would know the true life, look to Jesus.

But his life could be perfect only as it was given in sacrifice for man. His life was holy because it was a life sacrificed to God. No life can be possessed by God and used to his glory, that is not sacrificed to him. Jesus gave himself as an offering and sacrifice to God for us (Eph. 5:2). This left him without a body or human life through which to demonstrate moral principle to the world. But now comes the command to man, "I beseech you therefore, brethren, by the mercies of God, that ye present your bodies a living sacrifice, holy, acceptable unto God, which is your reasonable service." Rom. 12:1. God would have this human life of ours offered up in sacrifice, so that we are no more ours but his. When we do so, there will be a change, a great and wonderful change. That life will no longer be worldly or in the course of ordinary earthly-minded men. It will be a transformed life, a life in which God can live and do his will. Through the sacrifice of Christ, God will take the sacrificed life of man and possess it by his Spirit and again demonstrate moral principle to the world. O man, that is your calling in life. You are the vehicle to convey the perfections of God to an unbelieving world. Only an empty vessel for God to fill with himself and use to his glory.

O man, consider thyself, and know thyself, the purpose for which thou wert created, and the place which thou dost occupy in creation. Thou art no mean creature.

Thou art highest of all. God condescends to walk and talk with thee. He upholds thee in his hand. Angels minister to thee. When thou passest through the waters, God himself will be with thee so that they shall not overflow thee, and when thou walkest through the fire, he will walk with thee so that the flame shall not kindle upon thee; because thou art precious in his sight and honorable, and he has set his love upon thee. Thou art so precious to him that he gave his only begotten Son to die to ransom thee.

In the vast created universe, what place does man occupy? He stands out as a creature that bears the stamp of the divine image, a creature that is endowed with eternity. The heavens shall pass away, but man shall be forever. He was made capable of holding communion with the Creator. He occupies the relationship with God as child with parent. Being made in the likeness of God, he steps out upon the stage of the mighty universe to play the highest and noblest part in the entire drama of created existences. The songs of the morning stars as they sing together, pouring their anthems into the ears of God, are not such sweet music as is the voice of praise and adoration from the holy soul of man.

Man was created for the very highest purpose in the mind of God. He is chosen to represent the divine character. On the stage men and women represent certain characters. Man upon the great stage of life is selected to represent the holy character of God. Oh, that he might play his part well! He who occupies the highest and most responsible part in this wonderful play of the universe will sink to the lowest shame and disgrace if he fails. The eyes of earth, heaven, and hell were turned upon man as he stepped out to play his part. A garden eastward in Eden was selected as the ground of exhibition. It was whispered throughout the corridors of the universe, "Will he succeed? Will he play his part well?" Ah, the sad story! He failed and he fell, bringing a world into shame and disgrace, causing angels to weep and God to repent that he had ever made him.

But heaven's love was set upon him, and God sought a way whereby the fallen man could be lifted from his low, degraded plane to the high position he once occupied. After searching heaven through, God found but one way for man's redemption, but one price to pay. Would he pay it? He called his Son, his only Son, and pointed out to him the fallen condition of man, and how He was robbed of glory and devils were rejoicing. The Father said to his Son, "Only thy entering into that lower world in the likeness of sinful flesh and suffering and dying can redeem man." The Son replied, "I will go. I will suffer. I will lay down my life that man may be restored to his former position, so that he can again take up the part he was to play." The price was paid; the plan of man's redemption was effected; the divine image was again stamped upon the man, so that in Christ Jesus he could again come out and in his life's play reveal the character of God to the world.

Reader, this brings us down to your day and mine. We have our part to play in life. That part is to display the divine perfections. Through Christ this is possible. Oh, what responsibility! Will we play our part well? Again the eyes of earth, heaven, and hell are turned upon us. The apostle says, "We are made a spectacle unto the world, and to angels, and to men." 1 Cor. 4:9. "Men" includes both good and bad; likewise the term "angels" includes both good and bad angels. So, as I have said, earth, heaven, and hell are spectators. To live life as it should be lived is to act out our part upon the stage of life in such a way as to honor God and demonstrate his character before this mighty host of spectators.

Such is man. Through him the righteous character of God is made visible to the world. God himself is invisible; but since he comes into our heart and life, and since our life is physical and visible, his holiness becomes visible in our holy living. This is how to live. He who lives on a lower plane than perfect holiness is not living to God's requirements.

God did not redeem man at such a great price merely for man's sake. He redeemed him for his own glory. Redeemed man is God's purchased possession, that 'he should show forth the virtues of him who hath called him out of darkness into his marvelous light' (see marginal reading of 1 Pet. 2:9). Here again we learn that the mission of man is to show forth in his daily life the true, holy virtues of his Maker and Redeemer. This should be the first business of our life - living solely, purposely, and earnestly for God. We are beings in whom God dwells and through whom God is to display his own holy perfections. This is wonderful; this is weighty. There is, I repeat, great responsibility on man. But unless he feels it, he will never fill to the full the measure of life. Oh, how delighted is the loving heart of God to find in this world a being in whom he can dwell and through whom he can reveal his own beautiful life! Shall we yield ourselves to him? Shall we invite him into our hearts? Shall we consecrate our lives to him that he may hide our life in his life? Yes, dear Lord, we are thine, wholly thine, now and forever. Take full possession; live in us; reign in our hearts; use every faculty of our beings to thy own glory. Thy will be done in us and with us as it is done in heaven.

Jesus will gather his holy angels before him and address them thus: "Do you behold Brother -? He is a pilgrim and stranger down there in the earth. He is my child. I have washed him in my blood and clothed him with the beautiful garments of salvation. His heart is pure and full of love. He is dead to sin and the world. He loves my will, and his daily meat and drink is to do it. He loves my Word and has hid it in his heart. He keeps all my commandments. He seeks my glory. He often communes with me. He is fervent in spirit and zealous in good works. His good deeds and prayers I bottle up here in heaven, See that beautiful mansion yonder with its gates of gold and walls of jasper, its floors of transparent glass, its corridors of chalcedony, and colonades of topaz and beryl. That mansion is to be his home when his pilgrimage in that under-world is done. By his holy walk and devoted life he is now confessing me before men, and I take great delight in telling you that he is my child and in confessing him before you and my Father on his throne. Just as I have said in my Word, he that will confess me before men, him will I confess before my Father and the holy angels."

Redeemed man is a light in the world. In the darkness of this world he is a dispeller of gloom. His life shines, shedding its peaceful rays of light wherever he goes.

Man's life, when meeting the fullest purpose of God, is used as a magnifying-glass through which others may look and see the beauties of divine perfections. Alas! it is to be lamented that the life of many who profess to be followers of Jesus is such that it blurs the perfections of God.

In concluding this chapter, let me give you a few rules for daily living - rules which, if followed, will make your life a conveyancer of light, peace, and holiness from God to the world.

Live such a life that the pure and devoted will be pleased to have you come again.

Live so near to God that every man that meets you is made a little better by having met you.

Live such a life each day that the world can see in you the true way of life.

Be such a light that others can see the way to walk.

SOME USE TO JESUS.

O Christ, the way, the truth, the life,
Keep me safe mid the raging strife;
Help me a warrior brave to be
And take the battle-field for thee.

I fear not the swift arrow's power
Since thou art my high, strong-built tower;
The darts may have a bitter sting,
I shelter 'neath thy feathery wing.

Before me the Goliaths tall
Must quickly flee or headlong fall;
The foe is bruised beneath my feet;
In thee the victory is complete.

Jesus, to thee I give up all,
To live or die, to stand or fall.
The sparrows have thy kindly care;
I'm more than they, then need I fear?

I have a refuge from all harm
Within thy strong encircling arm;
Thou keepest me by day and night,
And guidest my weak steps aright.

The hairs on my unworthy head
Are numbered all, thy Book has said.

Gathered, like the defenseless brood,
My soul is kept in quietude.

As kind and loving parents would
Give to their children all things good,
So from thy presence angels bring
Unto thy child each needful thing.

Sometimes thou hidest thy sweet face;
The way is dark, I can not trace.
Thou doest best; I'll not repine,
But say, "Thy will be done, not mine."

Since them art good, so good, to me,
I beg to be some use to thee:
Intensify thy love divine
Within my heart, that I may shine

A little brighter, Lord, for thee,
That others thy great love may see.
Oh, crucified let all self be,
That thou mayst shine thy light through me.

I would not be so dazzling bright
That all the world might see my light,
But in some quiet nook of thine,
An out-of-way place, there I'd shine.

'Tis not for me to shine afar,
Like blazing sun or brilliant star;
Just help me at my door to be
A little candle-light for thee.

GODLY LIVING.

When some one is spoken of as living a worldly life, it is meant that he lives in a worldly manner, or in a manner like the world. Likewise, when some one is spoken of as living a godly life, it is meant that he lives in a godly manner, or in a manner like God. To many this is a hard saying, but it is possible for man to live just such a life; in fact, it is the only right way of life. A godly life is the only true life. Such a life is demanded by the Scriptures. We are to live "soberly, righteously, and godly in this present world" (Tit.2:12).

God's dear children are told to be "followers of him" (Eph. 5:1). In some translations this reads, "Be ye imitators of God," and in some others, "Be ye mimickers of God." From this we understand that to be a follower of God is to live or act in a manner like him. Again, it is said of those who abide in Christ, that they should walk even as he walked. Our manner of life should be as was the life of Jesus. It is said of Christ that "when he was reviled, he reviled not again." Although he was treated most shamefully by his enemies, he did not seek to avenge himself. When insulting remarks were made to him, he gave no reply. To live a godly life is to live in the same manner. When Christians are reviled, they bless; when they are persecuted, they suffer meekly and patiently. When Jesus was being put to death by his enemies, he prayed the Father to forgive them. When a man who had come to take Jesus had his ear cut off, Jesus in his tender compassion healed this bitter persecutor's wound. This is the true spirit of godliness.

The full standard of godliness is attained to only when the whole tenor of the life is in simplicity and godly sincerity. The apostle Paul said in testimony that his rejoicing was this: the testimony of his conscience that in simplicity and godly sincerity, not with fleshly wisdom but by the grace of God, he had had his conduct in the world. A godly life is wholly free from ostentation; every act is done in purest simplicity and truest sincerity. As God scrutinizes every act by his all-seeing eye, he discovers no impure motive, as vain-glory or lifting up of self; for all is in godly sincerity.

The grace of godliness in the Christian character is capable of cultivation and increase. There is a law in both the material and spiritual that exercise is conducive to growth. The Spirit-filled apostle said, "Exercise thyself unto godliness." In the Emphatic this reads, "Train thyself for piety." Here is something for every soul that has any aspiration to be more godly in life. Train yourself for piety. To become of deeper piety and more godly is the joy of the Christian heart. By training we become more pious. The lawn-tender forms an espalier by intertwining the branches of the vine. He keeps intertwining them as they grow, and by such training forms a latticework made of shrubbery. The soul intertwined with the meek and lowly life of Jesus will form a character of deep piety and sincere godliness. The daily life should be intertwined with the life of Jesus. Let there be no reaching out for anything outside of him. For a proper development of the Christian graces there must be a constant training or intertwining of the soul with God. This linking more tightly is the result of growth, and growth is produced by exercise, and exercise consists in reading the Scriptures, in prayer, and in deep thought or heart-communion with God. The athlete takes such exercises and eats such foods as will most properly develop and strengthen his muscles. The soul that has any longings for more of God must exercise to have its yearnings gratified. To be conscious of a growing up into Christ, to feel the soul intertwining more and more with the life of God, is fulness of joy and perfect happiness. Christian reader, is there an ardent flame of pure love in your heart? Do you walk with Jesus in a devout, trustful, reverential spirit? Do you oftentimes find your mind contemplating the wonders of creation and the glories of salvation? Is your soul habituated to breathe in the atmosphere of heaven deeply? Is that holy awe filling you? Is that tender sensibility of spiritual things filling your heart? Is that fine, keen edge upon your soul that gives such avidity for holy things? Is to become more godly a sincere desire of your heart? Then diligently perform all the duties that belong to a godly life. Some give great diligence for a time and make spiritual gain and then lose it all in a day of slackness. But do not slack, be constant, be persevering, be encouraged, reach forth, press forward, - and the prize of meekness, peace, and godliness will crown your life.

SOMETHING TO DO.

There is so much to do that every one is needed to help in doing it. In this great, busy world of life there is something for every one to do. The command is, "Whatsoever thy hand findeth to do, do it with thy might." Think over these words for a moment. Does not your heart feel that they imply great earnestness in life? They mean a life of labor - a life of service. "Do with your might" implies putting your whole heart into your work. Do it in just such a manner as shows you expect to make a success of it.

God has a work for every one that comes into the world. This world is going to be made a little better by your having come into it, or it will be made worse. Which shall it be? No one can do the work of another, since every one is given all he can do. It is true we are told to bear one another's burdens. I am to help you bear your burdens; that is a part of my work. You are to help me. We need the help of each other. But I can not do what you ought to do; for I have all I can do. What you neglect to do will have to go undone. If some one stops to do what you ought to do, just as large a rent is made in his life's work as would have been made in yours, but the reflection is on you.

A father who had five sons left them a certain work to do. He gave to each his portion according to his ability.

Upon his return he found that four of them had done their part and done it well, but one had only partially done his. Consequently, there was a neglected spot - a dropped stitch - which constantly showed itself. If we fail to do the work in life that God in his wisdom has assigned us, there will be in the Father's great plan a blank space, a neglected part, that will show through all eternity. Is your life or mine going to be the dropped stitch in the great web of human life? Down in our heart there is a No for an answer, is there not?

Let not the precious moments of your life flee away unimproved. Jesus is our example. He went about doing good. Everywhere he went, he left evidences that he had passed along that way. O pilgrim on life's journey, what are you leaving along the way to show in after-years that you have passed along? Is it flowers you are strewing? Is it sunshine to cheer and lighten the hearts of others? Sad indeed if there is none to say, "He did me good."

It matters not how small may be the part of his great work the Father has assigned you, do that little and do it well and do it with all the earnestness of your heart. It is your part, and you should do it with as much earnestness and interest as those who are engaged in the greater works do their parts. If your part is not done well, there will not be completeness in the divine plan. A single stitch dropped shows a blemish in the garment. In the sight of God the most menial task is as sacred as that of the highest order, and when well done as greatly meets his approval.

That is a beautiful thought expressed by the Mohammed Bible. It tells of Gabriel's being sent to earth to do two things. One was to keep King Solomon from becoming so much engaged with the affairs of his kingdom as to neglect the hour of prayer. The other was to give assistance to a little ant that was trying to bear its load of food up a hillside. To Gabriel the one duty was as important as the other because both came in the plan of God. "Whatsoever thy hand findeth to do, do it with thy might." Think these words over again. Let them have the full force of meaning to your heart. Take as much interest in helping the little child get the tangle out of the string as in building a church edifice.

Many are working, but alas! how few are doing their best! So much time and labor are being wasted; so many things are being done that had as well not be done. God wants not only our service but our best service. We are under obligation to do our best every day. If we let a day pass by without doing what we could and in the best way we could, our work is not perfectly done.

God pours his blessings out upon us, but the blessing is not to end with itself. Remember these words: "Freely ye have received, freely give." Seek to be blessed of God, that you may pass the blessing on to others. Leave some footprints here upon the sands of time, so that in after-years they may guide some one to a noble deed and better way. When you reach the end of life, you can experience no greater consolation than to know you have done what you could. Improve the moments of time while you have them. They are passing swiftly. They will not wait for you. Some people are going to do, but behold, the opportunity passes before they are ready. Opportunities do not wait. Do good while you may. You are going to give the flower tomorrow, but tomorrow the flower may have faded. You intended to speak a kind word yesterday, but thought you would defer until another day. But the strain was so great the life went out, and your kind word came too late. Today is the day to save the lost. Tomorrow may be too late. How sad that a soul through all eternity will be crying out, "You were going to help me, but you came too late." O God! help us to be up and doing while it is called today. What work you are going to do, do it now as the poet urges in the following beautiful lines:

"Let's not be living in the past,
  On what we have been doing,
Nor building castles in the air
  And after them pursuing.
'Work in my vineyard, go today':
  The Master's time is narrow
For yesterday we'll see no more -
  We may not see tomorrow.

"If for discouragements you look,
  You certainly shall find them,
But they are not discouragements
  Except to those who mind them.
The future for itself will care,
  We'll not its trouble borrow;
Sufficient evil is today,
  Then think not of the morrow.

"Let's cast our bread upon the flood,
  In many days to gather,
But then at eve hold out the hand
  For present blessings rather.
We hide the seed deep in the ground
  And watch the closing furrow,
When, lo! the field's already white,

Not waiting for the morrow.

"The sower and the reaper both
 May now rejoice together,
 For what they sow and gather in
 Is fruit that lives forever.
 The saint rejoices evermore,
 E'en in the midst of sorrow;
 He knows the weeping's but a night,
 Joy cometh on the morrow."

Man was made to labor. He is so constituted that he can not find true rest and enjoyment in idleness. How much the Bible says about good works! We are "created in Christ Jesus unto good works, which God hath before ordained that we should walk in them." Jesus purifies unto "himself a peculiar people, zealous of good works." We are told by the scriptures to "be careful to maintain good works" to "be not weary in well-doing," and to "do good unto all men." Time is given us to spend in usefulness, not in idleness. Money lost may be regained, but a moment never.

As Christians we have the mind of Jesus. With such a mind we can not be contented unless we are doing the will of God and making the proper use of the moments he gives us. Mind is the same quality whether it be in Jesus, in angels, or in men, and it is governed by the same laws. It is true that after man's transgression he was told that in the sweat of his face he should eat bread, but this does not imply that the disposition to labor is a result of the fall. The disposition to labor that we find in man's constitution is not the fruit of corruption in his nature, but is a part of his original constitution. We find this disposition in the mind of angels. They are ministering spirits. They are doing the will of God. How often we read in the Book that tells of heaven how angels have visited this transitory world of ours on errands of help, mercy, and consolation. They have closed the mouths of lions, opened prison doors, stilled the waves, whispered comforting words, rolled away the stone, and ministered strength and help to the needy.

Man is not designed for prayer and praise only; he is designed for service as well. His mission is twofold: he is to adore and praise his Creator and to serve his fellow men. Some have symbolized the two functions of man's life by the ascending and descending of the angels on the ladder that Jacob saw in his dream. They ascended to God and descended to man. Life should be spent in praising God and in serving man for God's sake.

There is something to do. There is much to do. There is too much to do for us to idle away one moment of time. A full and well-spent life is one which is spent in doing good out of pure love to God and man. When we shall have come down to the end of life's journey, how sweet it will be to know that we have done all we could to help other pilgrims make their journey in safety! There is a reward for every generous act. Heaven is faithful and will repay. What we do here will find an eternity of reward. Let not, therefore, one day pass you by without your doing something purposely for God.

SPIRITUAL DRYNESS.

We often meet with those who complain of dryness and deadness in their worship. They are very unlike the Psalmist's picture of the "blessed man." "He shall be like a tree planted by the rivers of water, that bringeth forth his fruit in his season; his leaf also shall not wither." This is a true picture of the Christian life. The soul should be as a watered garden - fresh and green and sparkling. It should be a springtime. You have seen a garden in the spring or one that is well-watered. All is beauty, freshness, and vigor. Such a garden is used by the prophet to symbolize the Spirit-filled soul. He says, "And the Lord shall guide thee continually, and satisfy thy soul in drought, and make fat thy bones; and thou shalt be like a watered garden, and like a spring of water, whose waters fail not." Isa. 58:11.

In order to have such a happy experience, however, the children of God must meet certain conditions. The context says, "If thou draw out thy soul to the hungry, and satisfy the afflicted soul." If our souls are not drawn out in pity for the hungry and we fail to do what we can to relieve them, we need not expect anything other than a spiritual drought in our own cases.

Spiritual dryness is sometimes the result of attachment to the world. "Set your affections on things above, and not on things on the earth." Unless we live by the

Bible, we can not be spiritual. A little affection for the things of earth robs the soul of spiritual life. In this matter Satan is an excellent reasoner. He will suggest that your desires are only for the glory of God; that you have no affection for the worldly object, but desire it only for God's glory. A young lady to whom I gave warning said that her desires were pure and that she had no affection for the object, but sought only to please the Lord. Very soon, however, she came to the realization that her soul was a desert place, and all because she had believed the falsehood of Satan. Beware how you desire earthly things for God's glory. Underneath may be a desire for self-gratification, ease, or luxury. If you are troubled by a lack of sensible devotion in worship, examine your affections. Possibly you may find some tiny roots twining around something of this world.

Spiritual dryness may be the result of sloth. "Slothfulness casteth into a deep sleep." Prov. 19:15. Spiritual idleness soon results in spiritual dryness. That sophism of Satan's, "No time for prayer," is very dangerous. Any neglect of spiritual devotion must result in lukewarmness. Oh, how unreasonable is man and how easily the desires of the flesh deceive! If you neglected to water your garden, you would not wonder for a moment why it was drying up. Then, when you are neglecting to water the soul in vigorous, spiritual exercises, why do you wonder at your being so spiritually dull? "Awake, thou that sleepest!" Up and away to the hill of the Lord. Be the frequent witness of a sunrise scene from the mount of prayer.

The San Jose scale works imperceptibly at first. Oftentimes its presence will be detected only by the experienced. Its presence will perhaps be known first by the fruit. If your spiritual fruit is not as beautiful, well-flavored, and fully developed as it should be, look for the presence of sloth in the soul. The poison of sloth will get into the soul little by little. First there will be a momentary delay of spiritual duties. Satan is too wise to suggest an entire abandonment of them, but he will suggest a little postponement. One delay will soon be followed by another and then by another. These delays are an opiate that dulls the spiritual senses, and thus they will yield more readily to postponements and finally find pleasure in them.

Let me make this still more simple, for some may need it made very easy to understand. When the soul is like a watered garden, it will be drawn to God in prayer in the early morning. Any delay will cause uneasiness and restlessness. The soul longs to hasten away to the presence of God. But one little delay after another brings on a morbid condition. The soul loses its keen relish; its senses become deadened, so that there is no uneasiness; while the senses of the self-life will find pleasure in sloth.

When the soul once gets into the habit of idleness, it experiences no little difficulty in getting out. On becoming aware of his state, the individual may acknowledge his inactivity and make half-formed resolves to be more earnest and diligent, only very soon to relapse into the same former sluggishness. This virus of sloth inoculates the entire spiritual being, poisoning the will and making spiritual activity most disagreeable. Not only does it destroy the will of the soul, but it blindfolds the eyes so that the individual can see no necessity for great fervency in spirit or for diligence in spiritual exercise. In a half-dazed manner he acknowledges that the "watchings often" and "fastings often" and "praying always" of the apostle Paul were very consistent in him, but does not realize that such would be as desirable in his own Christian profession. He wonders why he is not healed as people were in the days of Paul. Why wonder? He does not wonder why the flowers wither when it does not rain. It is the fervent, earnest prayer that God hears.

Nothing but the greatest diligence and determination and strong laying hold upon God will ever put spiritual sloth to death. In this respect it is like the South American animal called the sloth. Though one species of the sloth is only the size of a cat, and is extremely slow on the ground, its highest rate of speed there being not more than ten feet an hour, yet it is difficult to exterminate.

One reason why so many are slothful is that they do not realize the true worth of prayer. Oh, I would to God that men rightly valued communion with God or a few thoughts of him! The lifting of the heart to God in praise or adoration is of greater value than the wealth of worlds. It is not enough to know much about the doctrine of the Bible, to be acquainted with this present reform, and to live a fair outward life; we must be filled with the Spirit. We must be like a tree planted by the rivers of water, whose leaf does not wither. Take plenty of time to gain heaven. Take time to be spiritual. A home in heaven is worth laboring for. Work out your salvation with fear and trembling. Spiritual dryness is the result of spiritual indolence. Be active, and you will not be unfruitful.

PRAYER.

A work of this nature would be inexcusable for not saying something about prayer, for who can live life triumphantly without prayer? Who can properly estimate the true worth of prayer or rightly appreciate the privilege of prayer? Man esteems it a great honor to be admitted into the courts of the lords and kings of earth. What an honor it is to have audience with the King of glory! He extends the golden scepter to us, and we come hopefully, confidingly into his presence to tell him all that is in our hearts. He loves us so. We should not dare to come into the awful presence of the Great King did we not know that he loves us with an everlasting love. When we understand his love toward us, we tell him with joy and eagerness every desire of the heart.

Prayer is the energy and life of the soul. It is the invincible armor which shields the devoted Christian from the poisoned missiles shot forth from the batteries of hell. It is the mighty weapon with which he fights life's battles unto victory. He who lives in prayer reigns triumphant. The dark storm-clouds are driven away, mountains of discouragement are cast into the sea, chasms of difficulties are bridged, hope is given wings, faith increases, and joys abound. Hell may rage and threaten; but he who is frequent and fervent in prayer experiences no alarm.

By prayer the windows of heaven are opened, and showers of refreshing dew are rained upon the soul. It is as a watered garden, a fertile spot where blooms the unfading rose of Sharon and the lily-of-the-valley; where spread the undecaying, unwithering branches of the tree of life. By prayer the soul is nourished and strengthened by the divine life. Do you long for a brighter hope and deeper joy, for a deeper sense of the divine fulness, for a sweeter, closer walk with God? then live in prayer. Do you love to feel the holy flame of love burning in all its intensity in your soul? then enkindle it often at the golden altar of prayer. Without prayer the soul will weaken, famish, and die, the fountain of love dry up and become as a thirsty and parched desert. Do you admire the character Jesus? Behold his lowliness and humility, his gentleness and tender compassion. Have they any beauty and do you desire them to grace your soul? then draw them down from the skies in all their glorious fulness by the fervent prayer of faith. As through the process of assimilation food is transformed into an active, living being, so through the medium of prayer the character Jesus, in all its transcendent beauty and glory, becomes the character of man.

If you desire victory during the day, begin it with prayer - not a few hurried words, not a few ejaculations, but minutes of deep, intimate communion with God. Linger at the altar of prayer until you feel particles of glory drop in richness into your soul, scattering sweetness throughout. In the early morning hours, when the still, balmy breath of nature plays around you, let your soul fly away on the wings of prayer with its message of love and praise to its Maker.

"Sweet morning is the time to pray:

How lovely and how sweet
To send our early thoughts away
Up to the mercy-seat!"

If you desire to be more deeply and sincerely pious, pray. If you desire heights in his love, depths in his grace, fulness in his joy, and richness in his glory, pray, pray with all sincerity of heart and intensity of soul. Did you say you had no time for prayer? What a pity! Your happiness and success in life depend upon prayer. Your eternal enjoyment depends upon it. Then, oh, what a pity that you have no time for prayer! Satan will tell you there is no need of so much praying. He will give you indifferent feelings if he can, and tell you that you can get along well enough without it. He will do all he possibly can to prevent your praying. If there is not much benefit derived from prayer, why is he so concerned? The Bible commands are: "Watch and pray," "Pray always," "Be instant in prayer," "Pray without ceasing," etc. Beloved saints, I exhort you to a life of prayer. I beseech you in Jesus' name to go often into your closets and there in all earnestness of soul pray until the love of God and light of heaven fill your beings. Pray until a rapture from the skies sweeps over your soul, making the place of prayer the dearest spot on earth to you.

KEEP THE ROOTS WATERED.

How often you admire a tree for the loveliness of its green foliage and the profusion of its luscious fruit. You speak to your friend of the beauty of the tree and of the goodness of God in bestowing such a gift to men; but perhaps you do not speak nor even think of the coarse, unsightly roots hidden deep in the ground. But that tree owes its beauty and its life to roots. The foliage is bright and fresh and green because the roots are burrowing deep in a rich and well-watered soil. The flavoring of the fruit is generated by the roots down in the dark and silent chamber of the earth.

Perhaps there comes to your mind now some whose faces you always see lit up with a radiant glory. You can not fail to admire them. Their words contain a secret power and seem to awaken in you all that is noble. They seem to lift you into a higher life. From their words, their actions, and their countenances flows an influence that causes you to forget the things of earth and makes you feel as if you had joined the society of angels. Such ones have a secret hidden root-life that generates this peculiar charm in their visible life. Down in a closet is a secret laboratory where the fragrance and beauty and glory that flow out of their lives are compounded. There the roots of their inner life take hold upon the riches of heaven's grace and drink in of the waters that flow. In their oft and silent communion with God they take root downward, and then they go forth into life and bear fruit upward. While others are talking with their friends about the things of earth, they meet with God in the garden of graces, where the sweet spices flow out and the frankincense and myrrh scent the air, and there they become laden with a profusion of fruits and impregnated with a sweet odor, which they bear out into the world. They are like the tree planted by the rivers of water, whose leaf does not wither.

O beloved pilgrim, see that the roots of your inner being are well watered. Let them drink in the sparkling waters of life. Remember, effectual work for God consists more in being than in doing. Do not go about in your labor with an empty basket. It is only when you go out from deep and silent communion with God that your labor will be effectual. Never think that you have so much to do that you have not much time for prayer. An hour's work done in the quiet, secret power of the Spirit is worth more than a day of your own efforts. Keep the roots watered.

UNDER THE FIG-TREE.

In the beginning of his ministry Christ called to Philip to follow him. Upon being called Philip went in search of Nathanael to tell him that he (Philip) had found the Christ. Nathanael was somewhat doubtful, but at Philip's invitation he went to see. When Jesus saw Nathanael coming, he said, "Behold an Israelite indeed, in whom is no guile!" Nathanael, wondering how this man happened to know him, asked, "Whence knowest thou me?" Jesus answered, "When thou wast under the fig-tree I saw thee." John 1:48.

It is evident that something had occurred with Nathanael under the fig-tree outside the common details of every-day life. If there had not something rather unusual or something higher than the common events of life occurred there, the Savior would not have mentioned this one particular place. Any other place would have done as well. There was in this answer something that was highly significant to Nathanael. At this time there were many devout people looking for the "consolation of Israel." They were looking for the coming of the King of the Jews. It is not difficult for me to believe that Nathanael was under the fig-tree praying to God for the speedy coming of the Messiah. When Jesus said to him, "When thou wast under the fig-tree, I saw thee," Nathanael immediately replied, "Thou art the King of Israel." He was doubtless under the tree in prayer to this end not once only, but very probably for months and maybe for years. He had been praying for this very thing. He had selected one especial fig-tree as a place for prayer. It was not *a* fig-tree, but *the* fig-tree. There he had prayed long and often for Israel's King to come. So when Jesus said, "When thou wast under the fig-tree, I saw thee," he knew at once that his oft-repeated prayers were answered, and therefore said, "Rabbi, thou art the Son of God; thou art the King of Israel."

Many a devout one since that day has had his secret communion-place with God. Perhaps it was in the woods on a mossy knoll, under an oak, on a grassy spot on the bank of a stream, or under a shade-tree that grew by the brook in the meadow. To these places of solemn silence they would retreat when the shades of night were falling or when the light of the morning was streaking the sky, and there from the fulness of their souls they would pour out their praise and thanksgiving to God. These were the dearest places in the world to them. It may be there are aged ones today who had such places in the earlier days of their lives. Though they are now far removed from those scenes, these are still sacred in their memory.

There are those today who have their altars of prayer in some secluded place. There they meet God and tell him all their sorrows and cares, there they recount to him his loving kindness, there they implore his grace to sustain them through all their trying scenes of life, and there they worship at his feet. Bless his name! Beloved, have you a "fig-tree"? and are you often found under it? Have you a quiet nook somewhere which is hallowed by the presence of God?

The beloved disciple John, when in the Spirit, saw golden vials in the hands of the worshipers of the Lamb around the throne. These golden vials, he says, were "full of odors, which are the prayers of the saints" (Rev. 5: 8). Are you, dear reader, every day filling golden vials around God's throne with the sweet odor of prayer? Again, this disciple, when the seventh seal was opened, saw seven angels standing before God with seven trumpets. Then came another angel, with a golden censer. To him was given incense, which he offered with the prayers of saints upon the golden altar, and the smoke of the incense which came with the prayers of saints ascended before God. (See Rev. 8:3, 4.) We have the privilege of mingling our prayers with the incense that is being offered before the throne.

The Psalmist seemed to comprehend something of the nature of prayer when he said, "Let my prayer be set forth before thee as incense, and the lifting up of my hands as the evening sacrifice." Psa. 141:2. The prayers that were offered by the devout Cornelius were so fragrant before God that they were kept as a memorial of him. A memorial is something kept in remembrance of any one. If you want to be kept in remembrance before God, see that your prayers are highly impregnated with a sweet odor. You must pray or die. No one can retain spiritual life any great length of time without prayer. So we exhort you to a life of prayer.

SHUT THE DOOR.

It is as impossible to live and prosper spiritually without prayer as it is to live and prosper physically without food. Those who enjoy a close walk with God and have power with him are those who pray. Natural abilities and intellectuality can never supply any lack in spirituality. Unless you are spiritual, you are of but little use to God; and to be spiritual, you must live much in prayer. It is not those who are on their knees the oftenest or the longest that do the most praying. Some may pray more real prayer in one hour than others in two or three hours. Too many people leave the door open. Prayer that feeds the soul must be offered with the door shut. "But thou, when thou prayest, enter into thy closet, and when thou hast shut thy door, pray to thy Father which is in secret." Matt. 6:6.

God is in secret. He is hidden from the world. The world does not see him, neither knows him. You can never reach God in your prayers unless you shut out the world. Shutting the door means something more than closing the door of your literal closet. Persons may enter the literal closet and close the door, and yet have the world in their hearts and thoughts. Such have not closed the door in the true sense.

In the public assembly you must enter your closet

when you pray, and shut the door, or your prayers avail not with God. You must talk from your heart to the heart of God. Those assembled may hear your words, but they do not know the secret. The secret is between your heart and the heart of God. You scarcely hear your words. You know and hear more of the speaking of your heart. There is a blessing in such praying; there is a joy that can not be told. Such prayer feeds the soul upon the divine life and lifts us in realms of light and happiness. Thank God for the sweet privilege of secret intercourse with him. O beloved, when you pray, enter into your closet, and be sure to close the door.

ALONE WITH GOD.

This life of ours will never be all that it should be unless we are much alone with God. Only those who are oft alone with him know the benefit that is derived therefrom. You can not be like God unless you are much with him, and you can not live like him unless you are like him. The Scriptures tell us that Jesus departed into the mountain to be alone with the Father and that he was often "alone praying." When Jesus had anything of great importance to say to his disciples, he always took them aside from the multitude. When he was transfigured, he took three of his disciples into a mountain apart from all the world. When he was one time alone praying with his disciples, he asked them who he was. Peter answered, "The Christ of God" (Luke 9:18). It was only when he was alone with them and after prayer that he could bring them into such nearness to him that they might know in their hearts that he was the Son of God. When amid the active duties of life and when in contact with the world, we can scarcely come into that sacred nearness to God that will enable us to feel in our hearts all that God is. We may get slight glimpses of his glory, we may occasionally get a dim view of some of his beauty, we may feel a little warming of his love in our bosoms; but only when alone with him are we awed into wonder at the sight of his glory and great beauty. It is only then that we see him in his purity and feel the warm sunshine of his love. It is only then that our hearts can be deeply impressed with the knowledge that he is God, and in childlikeness we can look up to him and call him Father.

PRAYERFUL REMEMBRANCE.

At evening time when dark'ning shades draw nigh
And flickering rays of light go chasing by,
When all around glad nature sweetly sings
And seems you hear the sound of angel's wings,
Some one in memory may be brought to thee.

Maybe some one from distant land away,
Of whom you had no thought for many a day.
'Tis passing strange; you do not understand
Why such a one and from such distant land
Should step across the threshold of your mind,
Why he to you at this time should be brought.
'Tis mystery when all else claims your thought;
You seek to understand, but learn it not.

Maybe this one has conflict great and sore,
Is struggling long and hard 'gainst grim despair,
And God who rules the thought and mind of man
Has brought him this long way to you for prayer.
Then do not drive these whisperings from your mind
Nor cast them carelessly upon the wind:
'Tis but the voice of God, in tender care
For suffering one on life's broad way somewhere,
Inviting you to plead for him in prayer.

Kind friend, if at morning, noon, or night
I come to thee on wings of memory,

It is no doubt because the fight is fierce;
Then will you bow and pray to God for me?

HE CARETH FOR THEE.

Life will never be successful unless we learn to let God care for us. Unless we have faith to know that God is our keeper and that hence we have nothing to fear, we shall never be the cheer and sunlight in this dark world that God designed us to be. This is a world of trouble. Sin envelops many souls in awful midnight gloom. Some may never find Jesus unless they see him smiling in your face. You as God's dear child are to be a light to those poor, benighted souls. To be such a light, you must be full of light, and to be full of light you must be full of hope by faith in the cheering and encouraging promises of God. None can be truly happy, none can be the cheer, comfort, and consolation to the world, who are bearing their own burdens. Only those who have learned the sweet lesson of trust in God and know that he cares for them are truly happy and free and capable of cheering others.

> He who this one short life would live
> As heaven has designed
> Must scatter rays of cheering light
> From a heart with Hope enshrined.

There are many priceless promises in the Word of God. There is a promise for every need, condition, and circumstance of life. Among these blessed promises, here is one that has brought comfort to many a weary pilgrim on life's way: "Casting all your care upon him; for he careth for you." 1 Pet. 5:7. If this promise does not lift you far above all the trials, discouragements, and weariness of life, it is because you do not believe it nor understand the fulness of its meaning. "He careth for *you*." It is not your neighbor or your friend, but it is you. Cares will come to you, certainly; you could never cast your cares upon God if you had none. But you have them and doubtless many of them. The difficulty with many is, they do not cast them on God. Reader, your life will never be, it can not be, that free, happy, radiant, sunlit, helpful life that pleases God, if you bear your own cares.

There is nothing too trivial in life to take to God. In the very smallest concerns of your daily life he has an interest. In everything let your requests be known unto him. Do learn to take everything to him. Fret over nothing, never worry for a moment. Let nothing disturb or disquiet you. I say *nothing*. "He careth for you." Do you comprehend the full meaning of these words? Think them over for a moment. Let go of yourself and let God keep you. Oh, the freedom that belongs to the children of God! Theirs is a sweet land of liberty. But alas! how many will go on bearing their own burdens and weighted down with care with these words right before them: "He careth for you"! Why not let him?

Care is a grace-destroyer. If you would be strong in the grace of God, you must live free from care. It gnaws at the very vitals of the soul. A strong cable made of many fine wires was stretched across the river and was used to tow a heavy scow back and forth. One of the small strands was broken. This was thought to be a small matter. Soon another was broken and then another. Still this was not of much consequence. One by one more were broken but unheeded because each was so small. Finally all were broken, and the boat went adrift. A little care does not seem to be of much consequence. But the Bible says to be "careful for *nothing*," and to "cast *all* your care upon him."

Some have thought that the bearing of burdens and cares made us strong in the Lord. No, it is the casting of them on Jesus that makes us strong. For a man to be down under a heavy weight is no exercise to his muscles; but to be up on his feet and passing heavy weights on to another, this is exercise. To be down under burdens and cares is no exercise to the soul, but is really death; the passing of the cares on to Jesus is the exercise and the strength of the spiritual powers. If you only knew how much grace a little care destroyed, you would quickly cast them on Jesus. Some have come to find themselves entirely without grace because they did not cast their cares on the Lord. We knew a sister whose baby was such a care that she could not keep saved. One day when asked how she was getting along in the Lord, she answered, "Not well; the baby is such a care and worry that I can not keep the victory I should like to have." Was it not too bad to lay such a blame upon a poor little innocent child? I was asked one time if it was possible to reach an experience where we would never fret or worry. Certainly we can. We shall never get to a place where we shall have no temptations, but we can get to a place where we shall not yield to the temptations. Your life has not reached that degree of perfection that it should, until you have attained to such an experience. Jesus says, "Take no thought for the morrow." When you are having any great anxieties about future things, you are doing what Jesus tells you not to do, and you can not do something he tells you not to do without suffering spiritual loss. Oh! why will you worry about anything, when Jesus says, "Be anxious for nothing." "But," you say, "when there is no meat in the larder and no flour in the bin, can we then be not anxious?" There are those who have been in just such circumstances and yet have not been greatly troubled.

If you will be over-anxious about anything, you can never live close to God. When anxieties knock at the door of your heart for admittance and you open the door and let them in, you are opening the door to a dangerous band of robbers. They are robbers of grace and peace. When anxieties step over the threshold of your heart's door, grace and peace fly out of the window. "But what am I to do?" sighs a care-worn soul. Do just what a good man says he did. He said that he opened his heart to Jesus, and he came in and shut the door. Let Jesus keep the door of your heart. When anxieties come and want into your heart, tell them they must get permission from Jesus, because you have given your whole heart up to him. This is what is meant by "casting your care upon him." It is not enough to kneel down and ask Jesus to take them; you must cast them upon him. In this is the soul's needed exercise. The soul that will do this shall be strong. You must put the burden over on the Lord's shoulders and let him bear it. He will bear all your burdens for you if you will lay them upon him.

Not only must you put them upon him, but you must let go entirely. You do not even need to look after them to see what he does with them. Your little child comes to you with a tangled cord. It gives it over into your hands, but holds to one end. Now, you know that in order to get the tangle out, you must have both ends.

O weary one, Jesus will disentangle all the cares of life, but you must let him have both ends. He does not want your help. You hinder him if you attempt to help him. Cares will come; things that are of a trying nature will assail us as long as we live; but we have a refuge in Jesus; he will bear our burdens; he will care for us.

CONSIDER THE LILIES.

What a beautiful lesson Jesus has taught us of rest and quietness from the lilies! "Consider the lilies of the field," he says, "how they grow: they toil not, neither do they spin." He is trying to teach us how free we can be - free from all earthly cares and anxieties. The lily does not struggle; it has no anxieties about its future; but it grows. It grows to be beautiful. Even Solomon in all his glory was not arrayed like one of them. God paints the flower with greater beauty than the robes of kings. If you would be beautiful, you must rest in the Lord. Just a little struggling, and you will mar the whole. Christ wants to reveal himself through you. He will shine the beauty of his own glorious person into your soul if you will but be quiet. Have no anxieties about the things that pertain to this life, and Jesus will clothe you with the beauties of heaven. Character, as the years pass on, is revealed on the face. The miser's face shows the miserly condition of his heart. Jesus will stamp his own image upon the soul if the soul is kept in quietness, and this image will stand out in beauty on the face and outward life.

By this lesson of the lilies Jesus did not mean to teach that we should not pray. He once said, "Men ought always to pray." We must pray much. If we do not pray, Satan will have us toiling and spinning. Keeping close to Jesus with a strong faith and a firm trust is the only way to rest, and we can not do this without much prayer. "Cease thy toiling and care." Learn a lesson from the lilies. Rest in the Lord, and he will make you an object of Christian beauty that will bless the world. Even after you are long gone, that restful, patient life will cast its rays of light and beauty back and chase away the shadows from the life of others.

> The day has gone, the twilight fades,
> There's stillness everywhere;
> I seek some place of solitude,
> And humbly bow in prayer.
>
> I tell the story of the day -
> The joy, the grief, the care;
> I keep not back one secret thing,
> But tell it all in prayer.
>
> O heart of mine, be light and free,
> Not lightest burden bear,
> In everything let thy requests
> Be told to God in prayer.
>
> Yes, all; I tell it all to Christ
> In evening twilight dim:
> Somehow my heart much lighter grows
> Since all is told to him.
>
> I lay my life at his dear feet -
> O Jesus, I am thine!
> I'll walk the way of life with thee;
> Thy will, O Christ, is mine.
>
> And now I lay me down to sleep
> While gathering shadows fall,

And sweet indeed my rest shall be,
Since Jesus knows it all.

SORROWFUL YET ALWAYS REJOICING.

This world is sometimes called "the vale of tears." Jesus said, "In the world ye shall have tribulation," but he also said, "In me ye shall have peace." The way to heaven is through tribulations. Those whom John saw standing before the throne and the Lamb arrayed in white robes and with palms in their hands, were one day where we now are, and thank God, we, coming up through great tribulation, shall some day be where they are. While man in this world will meet with sorrow, he can by the grace of God always rejoice. Alum thrown into muddy water will clarify it. The grace of God thrown into a cup of sorrow will turn it to joy. Sorrows are needful. It is only a barren waste where there is no rainfall.

We have sung, "No days are dark to me." This can indeed be true, but it is not to be taken in the sense that there will be no clouds nor rainfall. Show me a man who never has a cloud to float across his sky, and I will show you a man who has not faith enough to see clearly in the sunlight. It is those whose faith pierces through the cloud and keeps the smiling, sunlit face of Christ in view that have the truest, sweetest joy. Their rejoicing is in the Lord. By bravery and force of will some may shut themselves against sorrow and soon become insensible to it. But the heart that is steeled against sorrow is in all probability so calloused that it can not experience joy. Those who know the deepest sorrow may ofttimes know the fullest joy, and that in the midst of their sorrow. Do not harden your heart against sorrow, but look to Jesus for that balm which heals, that grace which sustains, that comfort which gladdens. Some have thought that true joy consists in never having a sorrow; that those who have sorrow have not found the way of peace. In this they err. Those who never have a sorrow rejoice because they have no sorrows, but some who have sorrow have learned to rejoice in the Lord. This is truest joy.

"Sorrowful," said one who was crucified with Christ, "yet always rejoicing." He never once denied having sorrow; nay, he said, "I have great heaviness, and continual sorrow in my heart." But he also said, "I glory." It was the deep sorrow that made him most like Jesus. He had feeling. "We sorrow," he said, "but not as those who have no hope." The world knows a sorrow that the Christian does not know. Christians should be careful lest in hardening themselves against feeling they do not render themselves incapable of feeling compassion, sympathy, and pity.

Let the tears flow. If you keep them back, the fountain will dry up. May the Lord pity those who have no tears! Jesus wept. The apostle Paul said, "Out of much affliction and anguish of heart I wrote unto you with many tears." Oh, that unfeeling heart that can not suffer, that dry heart that has no fountain of tears! It weeps not over the sorrows of others and consequently can not rejoice when others are joyful. Only those who weep can truly rejoice.

You rejoice because you and your family are in good health, because your friends are smiling upon you, because circumstances surrounding you are favorable, because you have an abundance of good things to eat and of clothing to wear. But your rejoicing is only in earthly things. We are to be grateful for these things, but they are only the sea-foam of joy; the water lies beneath. True joy is to rejoice not only *in* the Lord but *with* the Lord. Rejoice in those things in which Jesus and the angels rejoice. When your goods are being wasted, you find your deepest joy because God is being glorified.

If you can not weep with angels, you can not rejoice with them. See that aged pilgrim: his has been a hard and stony way; loved ones have gone one by one from his embrace; riches have taken wings and flown away; sorrows are multiplied; trials are many; burdens are heavy; he is footsore, sad, and weary. Angels are bending over him weeping. Can you weep with him and them? They comfort him. The sadness of his heart begins to die away; hope begins to dawn. The dawning of the hope causes the angels to rejoice. This is truest joy. Rejoice when souls are saved; rejoice when hearts are gladdened; rejoice when God is praised. This is the true source of purest joy. But it is only those who are capable of suffering deeply with the sufferings of others, that can truly rejoice when their sufferings are turned away. The more we are like Jesus, the more we have of his Spirit, the tenderer will be our hearts and the more deeply will our souls be moved by the sufferings of others.

When some dear friend has proved untrue; when some loved one has gone astray; when the death-angel has left a chair vacant at your hearth-stone and deep sorrow lies upon your soul, then it is that you feel nearer to Jesus. You feel ripe for heaven. The world has suddenly gone out, and you have cast your eyes upward. Do not try to keep back the tears; let them flow. They are pearls in angels' sight. It is the tears of the child that touches the heart of the parent, and cites him to give comfort to the little one. It is the tears of the Christian that touches the great loving heart of God and moves him to give that solace which only Heaven gives. David said in a time of deepest sorrow - his son was seeking his life - "It may be the Lord will look on my tears [margin], and that the Lord will requite me good." Hezekiah was doomed to die. The prophet told him to 'set his house in order, for he should die, and not live.' The dying man turned his face to the wall and prayed, "I beseech thee, O Lord, remember now how I have walked before thee in truth and with a perfect heart, and have done that which is good in thy sight"; and he "wept with a great weeping [margin]." This touched the heart of God, and he said, "I have heard thy prayer, I have seen thy tears: behold, I will heal thee."

If the heart of God's saints were a deeper fountain of tears, more sick people would be healed in these days. Around are the sick and suffering, but alas, how few tears! When saints have so deepened into God, cultivated such a tenderness of heart, and become so deeply compassionate, that they will "water their couch with their tears all the night" at the sight of sick persons, they will get answers to their prayers. To such God will say, "Behold, I will heal him." If tears will not reach God, the case is hopeless. Esau sought for a place of repentance and sought it with tears, but could not find it. The mentioning of tears here implies that the addition of tears to earnest heart-seeking has influence with God. Jeremiah, in his lamentations for fallen Israel, said, "Oh, that my head were waters, and mine eyes a fountain of tears, that I might weep day and night for the slain of the daughter of my people!" He knew that if anything would avail with God, it would be tears therefore he wished that his eyes were a fountain of tears, so that God might be moved to save Israel.

"They that sow in tears shall reap in joy." There can be no harvest from seed sown unless the seed is watered. As you go out to sow seed in the Master's field, water them with your tears if you would have a joyful harvest. May God save his people from unfeelingness of heart! A soul with no tears is a soul with no flowers. There is no verdure where there is no water. Those who are not deep enough in God to shed tears over a lost and ruined world are not deep enough to shed tears of joy over a soul's salvation. Out from the depth of his heart Jesus cried, "O Jerusalem, Jerusalem! how oft would I have gathered thee as a hen gathereth her brood under her wing, but ye would not." When did you shed tears over lost souls? Do you ever have a Gethsemane? Is your pillow ever dampened by tears shed for a doomed world? Do you ever go out beneath the starry sky and with outstretched arms cry in the severe pains of travail, "O lost souls, lost souls! how oft would I have gathered thee to Jesus, as a hen gathers her brood under her wing, but ye would not"? Only those who have deep travail of soul for the lost can fully rejoice when the lost are found.

One of the apostles said he served the "Lord with many tears." A heart from which flows no tears is not a heart that is wholly imbued by the Spirit of God. Tears of compassion for the suffering, tears of warning and entreaty for the lost, tears of joy for the saved, will flow through a perfectly holy heart as freely as water through a sieve. Sunlight perforates the block of ice from the center outward; so the love of God perforates the heart to its depths and lets the tears of affection, pity, and sympathy flow out.

Do not try to escape suffering. Do not shut your heart against sorrow. It is the bruised flower that gives out the sweetest scent. Open thy heart to God and let him bruise it, let sorrow flow in and break it, that sweetness may flow out. When the poet sang:

"I no trouble and no sorrow
See today, nor will I borrow
Gloomy visions for the morrow,"

he sang not of sorrow for souls lost in sin, nor of needful heaviness through manifold temptations, nor of sorrow awakened by the suffering of others, but of that sorrow which arises from the world through distrust and separation from God.

There is a sorrow which comes through Christ. It is as the refiner's fire, purifying the soul and binding it closer to God. Such sorrow detaches the heart from the world and from self, and hides it in God. It is impossible for the soul to approach any degree of nearness to Christ only through sorrow and suffering. In my own experience my heart once longed for deeper grace. My whole soul breathed out, "O Jesus! give me more meekness." For a few days a heavy cloud of sorrow lay upon me; when it had passed away, I had an answer to my prayer.

I would have you beware of that unfeeling state in which one has no sorrow, and mistakingly attributes its absence to grace. Grace helps us bear sorrow, but does not harden our hearts against it. Sorrow brings us to a throne of grace for grace and grace brings us joy, so that we have joy in sorrow. No other joy is so sweet as this. It is the real and true joy of Christ.

GENTLENESS.

Fruit-bearing trees are used in the Scriptures to represent the race of mankind. The Savior likens the wicked to "corrupt trees," which bear evil fruit and the righteous to "good trees" which bear good fruit (Matt. 7:15, 20). He also teaches very emphatically the impossibility of one's being a good tree and yet bearing evil fruit, or of being a corrupt tree and bearing good fruit. Since the nature of the fruit we bear determines what manner of tree we are, it is very advisable that we as professing Christians should frequently examine the fruit we are bearing. To be Christ's, or to be a Christian, we must have the Spirit of Christ; for the Scriptures say that "if any man have not the Spirit of Christ, he is none of his" (Rom. 8:9). As certainly as cause produces effect, those who have the Spirit of Christ bear the fruit of the Spirit. Not to bear the fruit of the Spirit is full proof that you have not the Spirit. Then a close examination of the fruit you are bearing will reveal to you whether or not you have the Spirit of Christ, whether or not you are his, whether or not you are a Christian. You can make a superficial examination, and allow yourself to be deceived. You can make excuses for yourself because of your weaknesses, and thus deceive yourself. But a close, thorough, profound examination will disclose to each one the manner of spirit he is of.

Gentleness is one of the fruits of the Spirit (Gal. 5: 22). If we have the Spirit of Christ, we bear this fruit. "Well," says one, "in my very make-up I am rough, harsh, and hasty." You need to be made anew. When God finds a man that is rough, harsh, and severe in his make-up, He will, if the man will yield to the operation of the Holy Spirit, make him mild, gentle, and peaceful. People go to a hospital and by a scientific operation have abscesses and tumors removed from the stomach and other internal parts. God, by a blessed, wonderful, and successful operation of the Holy Spirit, will take that roughness, harshness, and severity out of your nature, and instil mildness, tenderness, softness, and gentleness instead. Harshness and roughness are a corruption that God, in his gracious plan of salvation, is pleased to remove. If you will allow the Holy Spirit to work in you that which is pleasing in God's sight, he will make you gentle.

What is gentleness? It is blandness, softness, mildness, and meekness. It is the opposite of harshness, roughness, etc. It is sweetness of disposition, mildness of temper, softness of manner, kindness, tenderness, etc. Those who are of a gentle disposition act and speak without asperity. They are not morose, sour, crabbed, and uneven, but are smooth, mild, and even. Good manners are intimately connected with gentleness, and good manners are no dishonor to Christianity.

The apostle Paul by way of testimony said to the Thessalonian saints, "We were gentle among you, even as a nurse cherisheth her children." 1 Thess. 2:7 Such was his manner. As a kind mother is to a delicate child, so was he to those whom he loved. Vastly different was he then from what he was when he was persecuting and wasting the church of God. He had been changed by grace. He exhorts servants of the Lord to "be gentle unto all men" (2 Tim. 2: 24) and to be "gentle, showing all meekness unto all men" (Tit. 3:2). David, in his sublime tribute of praise to God in 2 Sam. 22: 36 says, "Thy gentleness hath made me great."

Would you, my reader, like to be more gentle in your manner? Are you too harsh and rough? Are you, if a parent, as gentle to your children as you should be, at all times? Husband, are you as kind and gentle toward your wife as you should be? Do you believe you fill the Bible measure in this particular? Are you as gentle to your domestic animals as you should be? or do you have impatient feelings and act in a hasty, abrupt manner towards them? If you meet with something quite provoking from your wife or the children or the animals, do you keep as mild and sweet as you know you should? Now, I hope you will examine closely. I do not mean to condemn you; I want to help you. There are many professing saints today who are not nearly so gentle as they should be. Why not be in earnest, and seek God for help, and make improvement? Why go along with crossness, and coldness and snappishness in your life? Be gentle toward all.

Gentleness is a beauteous grace. Her excellence is great. By culture this grace is capable of much improvement. Too few saints experience it to the extent they should. I beseech you by the gentleness of Jesus to be in earnest and improve upon your gentleness. Never allow a frown or a scowl to settle for a moment upon your brow. It will leave its mark if you do so. Learn to be gentle in your home. Sometimes when far away from home, you picture to yourself how gentle and kind and loving you should be at home. By

God's grace you can be just as gentle as you see in the picture you should.

TENDERNESS.

In order for life to be what it should, it must flow from a heart full of tenderness. This is that quality of soul which enables us to give kind attention to others, to be willing and eager to do good, to exercise great carefulness to give no offense, and to be soft and gentle in every expression. Like all other good qualities, this is found in perfection in the character of God. "The Lord is very pitiful and of tender mercy." Because of his pity he never lays upon his trusting child a greater burden than he can bear, and in his tender mercy he always gives to each trial a happy ending.

It will be helpful to study for a few minutes the principle of tenderness as an attribute in the nature of God. "Like as a father pitieth his children, so the Lord pitieth them that fear him." It is the father who sees his little child in deep pain that knows what pity is. It is that feeling which makes the father desirous of bearing all the pain. It was the pity or compassion of God for the lost in sin that caused him to give his only Son to suffer and die for them. When God saw the wretchedness of men, he had such a feeling in his heart that he could find relief in no way but in providing the only means of their rescue. Oh, think of this! The child of God never has a pain or a sorrow but that God has a feeling of pity. The knowledge that some one has pity for us and fellowships our suffering goes far toward alleviating our pains. Recently while I was in deep soul-suffering, I received a letter containing these words: "We suffer in spirit with you." This was a great relief. If in a time of trial we could know how God was suffering with us, it would be a great consolation.

Again, we read, "As one whom his mother comforteth so will I comfort you; and ye shall be comforted in Jerusalem." Who is it that knows not the comfort of a mother? When we hear of a young man's meeting with a sad accident away from home, we have great pity; but when we learn of his mother's having gone to him, we feel better. Ah, the comfort of a mother is surpassed only by the comfort of Jesus. "If Mother were only here!" says the troubled daughter. Nothing else so fittingly represents the nature of the comfort that God gives as the comfort of a mother. O child of God, you will never have a sorrow nor a pain but that the tenderness of God will cause him to come and comfort you. Let us lift up our hearts and praise him for his mercy and comforting love. A mother may forget to comfort her child, but God will never forget.

The tenderness of God is revealed in these touching words: "How often would I have gathered thy children together as a hen gathereth her chickens under her wings." The imagery is homely, but oh! so impressively sublime. I can not do better than to use here the words of another. "Was ever imagery so homely invested with such grace and such sublimity as this at our Lord's touch? And yet how exquisite the figure itself of protection, rest, warmth, and all manner of conscious well-being in those poor, defenseless, dependent, little creatures, as they creep under and feel themselves overshadowed by the capacious and kindly wing of the mother bird. If wandering beyond hearing of her peculiar call, they are overtaken by a storm or attacked by an enemy, what can they do but in the one case droop and die, and in the other submit to be torn to pieces? But if they can reach in time their place of safety under the mother's wing, in vain will any enemy try to drag them thence. For rising into strength, kindling into fury, and forgetting herself entirely in her young, she will let the last drop of her blood be shed out and perish in defense of her precious charge, rather than yield them to an enemy's talons. How significant all this of what Jesus is and does for his helpless child!" Under his great wing he tenderly, lovingly gathers his little ones and there they are secure. He is a safe retreat.

From the song of Moses we learn still more of God's tender care. "As an eagle stirreth up her nest, fluttereth over her young, spreadeth abroad her wings, taketh them, beareth them on her wings: so the Lord alone did lead him, and there was no strange god with him." This metaphor beautifully expresses the care and the tenderness of God toward his children. The eagle is noted for her great attachment to her young. Her care is extraordinary. When the little eaglets have attained age and strength to leave the nest and learn to fly, the mother bird bears them up, when weary, on the top of her wing.

These all express to our hearts the wonderful tenderness of God to his children. But there is nothing in the material world that forms a full and perfect analogy for the things in the spiritual world. These are too high.

If we do not have the tenderness of God in our hearts,

our life comes short of being a full and true life. The Bible tells us to "be kind one to another, tenderhearted." There is no true holiness of life without tenderness. As we get deeper into God, we become more tender of heart.

There are some things that will prevent this tenderheartedness. Just a little feeling of resentment, a little desire for retaliation, or a secret wish for something to befall those who have done us an injury will callous the heart and harden the affections. When we have been slighted by some one or misjudged, oh, how Satan strives to get us to thinking much about this, and to work a "hurt" feeling into our heart. Even to think about the meanness of others will bring a harshness and coldness into the inner life. That which we condemn in others will, if we think and talk much about it, creep into our own hearts.

You say you are saved and sanctified. Thank God for such a blessed experience; but you have much yet to gain. You have not yet attained to the full depth of anything. There is yet a tenderness of heart you can reach only through many and varied experiences. There is tenderness of voice, tenderness of manner, tenderness of feeling, tenderness of thought, you will attain to only through much and deep communion with God. It is those intimate and familiar talks with Jesus that fashion us into his glorious image. A brother minister related to me a few mornings ago his experience of the night before. He lay awake, he said, for a long time and had a sweet talk with the Lord. So intimate was the communion that, turning over to go to sleep, he said, half unthinkingly, "Good night," as if parting from a dear friend. Such close union with Jesus gives us clearer visions of his character and stamps his beauty upon our souls.

Have you not seen those who are harsh, rough, and unfeeling in their speech and manner. No one wants to be like them. We are glad to get away from them. They measure a person by their standard, and if he is not what they think he should be, they speak about him in an unloving and unfeeling manner. We feel that something coarse and flinty needs to be taken out of their nature. We do not say they are not sanctified, but they are too bitter and severe. They need to be bathed in the love of God; they need to be immersed in the sea of his gentleness. We have seen, on the other hand, those who were so feeling, so quiet, tender, and gentle, that their presence was like the breath of a sweet spring morning. There was a tenderness in their eye, a softness in their voice, a pathos in their feeling, that cast over your soul a sense of delight.

There is much for us to gain. But we can gain it only at the end of the bayonet. If we would win, we must fight. There is no victory without battle. One brother, after gaining a decisive victory, said, "The devil is dead." He was so victorious and free that he thought the devil must be dead. In a short time, however, the brother learned his mistake. The prince of the power of the air still lives, and we still have our humanity. If we are not prayerful and watchful, we become disposed to contend for our way; to feel a little bitter if we are trampled upon. Jesus tells us to "resist not evil." We are not only to not resist evil outwardly, but to have no resisting feeling in our hearts. If we would have holiness of life, we must have tenderness of spirit. If you desire your life to be like the oasis in the desert, where the weary traveler is refreshed, be tender of heart, be compassionate, bear every trial with patience, endure all suffering without a murmur, commune much with God, and he will bring you out into that tenderness of soul that will make your life, everywhere you go, like the atmosphere of heaven.

THE CHRISTIAN WALK.

Life is termed a walk in the Scriptures. Where they say that we ought to walk as Jesus walked, they have reference to our manner of life. The way in which a Christian walks is called the way of life. It is called the way of life because it leads to a land of life - a place where death never enters, where all is life, and life forevermore. The Christian walks in the way that leads to that land of life. There is also a place of death, and the way there is called the way of death.

The way along which the Christian walks is a narrow way. "Strait is the gate, and narrow is the way, that leadeth unto life." But we need have no fear; for although it is narrow, it is not dark. "Thy word is a lamp unto my feet, and a light unto my path." I would rather walk in a narrow way in full light than in a broad way in the dark. The Word of God lights up the Christian's pathway. How beautifully the electric lights light up the walks in the city park! There is no danger of stumbling. The Bible is a light along the way of life, and it lights the way beautifully. Not one step need be taken in the dark. There is light for every step of the way. Sometimes the Christian may think he has reached a dark place; but if he will open his Bible, he will find a light to lighten that very spot.

THE CHRISTIAN IS TO WALK CIRCUMSPECTLY.

"See then that ye walk circumspectly." Eph. 5:15. To walk circumspectly is to walk cautiously; to look where one is stepping; to be vigilant, watchful, diligent, attentive. Be our pathway ever so light, if we do not look where we are stepping, we may stumble. Conybeare and Howson render the above text in these words: "See then that ye walk without stumbling." We are to walk not as foolish people but as wise. We would say that the man acts foolishly who does not look at all in the way he is walking. Those who are wise in business walk carefully; they look where they are going; they take advantage of every opportunity to make their business a success. In our Christian walk we are to seize upon every opportunity to make progress. There is no time in this short life for ease. Carelessness and indolence are dangerous and destructive to spirituality. An indolent man will never accomplish much for God nor be of any great benefit to his fellow men. But oh, how easy to become careless!

Many begin the Christian walk in carefulness and diligence, but soon give place to carelessness and neglect. How prone people are to lose interest in anything when the new has worn away! They take great interest in the new preacher, but they will become so familiar with him and so accustomed to him that they will lose interest. They have never heard any one preach so well as the new preacher, and what he says has such weight and authority; but behold, after the new has worn away, he can not preach any better than any other they have no more regard for his words than they have for the words of others. There is an old adage which says, "A new broom sweeps clean." The boy is eager to cut wood with the new ax. A child will carefully write like the copy for the first few lines; but the farther down the page, the greater the carelessness. The young lady takes great interest in the music lessons at first; she wants to practise all the time; but it soon gets old, and then it is hard to keep up an interest. The husband is very loving, kind, and attentive to his wife for a while; but alas! in a little while she becomes old to him, and then he lets her shift for herself. This need not and should not be; but it seems to be the nature of man.

In the Christian life there is a strong tendency to let things run down. Some persons hear a sermon and they are awakened, but they are soon lulled to sleep again. Perhaps the example of some one has shown them that they do not pray enough, and they resolve to pray more, but they soon drift into the same careless way. Maybe they see that they do not read enough and improve themselves, and they are greatly stirred to do better, but alas! how soon they allow that resolution to weaken and become as negligent as ever. Nothing but the greatest diligence and unyielding determination will save us from getting weary in welldoing. Keep up a strong faith. Hold your mansion in the skies well in view and let nothing hinder you in your journey home.

There are professed Christians who, I am sorry to say,

never take a good look at their mansion in heaven, and it is to be feared that many who are really God's children do not view their home above as often and distinctly as they should. They see more of temporal things than of eternal things. It is by faith that we see eternal things, but if we have too keen a vision for temporal things, it dims our spiritual vision. If you knew you had a fine home in an adjoining State, and you had never seen it, you would want some one who had seen it to give you a description of it. Perhaps you would want a photograph of it. You would take a look at the picture often, and would learn all about it you could, and would think of the time when you could go and live there. Now, Jesus tells you that he has prepared a mansion for you in heaven. He does not tell you much about it, but you know full well that a mansion that Jesus prepares is perfect and complete. Why not think much about this mansion? why not view it often by faith? why not learn all about it you can? Getting too much engaged with the things of this life is the reason why. To walk circumspectly is to see that every step bears us heavenward, to have our faces set toward God, to have our eternal home in view, and to be journeying that way. We are not to be sauntering along, but to be industriously living for God and heaven.

How often have you decided that you would be more prayerful, would read more, would love God more, and the souls of men, would do more for the cause of God! How often you have decided to walk more worthily of God, to be more patient, to live a higher life, to be slower to speak, to cultivate a spirit of love and kindness, to be more like Jesus! You started out well and with great diligence, but alas! ere long you became weary in well-doing; you became less vigilant; you did not walk so carefully and were less attentive to your way. One day a circumstance occurred that caused a brother to see that he was not as attentive to others as he should be and let many opportunities of helping others in little things go by unimproved. He decided that he would be more watchful, and thus be more helpful; but, as he said, he soon became as negligent as ever. Time after time he resolved and as often became negligent. Do not be discouraged. A little more determination, a little more faith in God for help, and you will triumph.

THE CHRISTIAN'S WALK A WALK WITH GOD.

"He hath showed thee, O man, what is good; and what doth the Lord require of thee, but to do justly, and to love mercy, and to walk humbly with thy God." Micah 6:8. The life of Enoch is descriptive of the Christian's life, and it is said that he "walked with God." Hand in hand with God, heart in heart, and life in life, is the true Christian way. In order to walk thus with God, we must be in agreement with him; for two can not walk together heart in heart unless they be in agreement. To be agreed with God implies submission to the divine will. It is to go where he leads.

"He leadeth me" is the sentiment of the Christian heart. He may sometimes lead in a laborious path; nevertheless we go. He may lead in a way that brings suffering and self-denial; he may take our loved ones from us; he may call somebody dear to us to a foreign field, or he may call us. If we would walk with him, we must not draw back, but say, "Lord, thy will be done. I will go with thee all the way." Such a walk may lead over some thorny paths and through some waters and fiery trials, but it pleases God and ends in heaven, So onward let us go.

THE LATEST IMPROVED.

As we walk along the streets of villages and cities, we see machines of different kinds exposed to view and bearing a card with these words: "The Latest Improved." For our life to be perfect every day, it must be our latest improved. The world is getting worse, we say, but you and I as Christians can daily grow better. Our life today can be an improvement over our life of yesterday. The Christian life is a real life, and is as capable of development as any life. The same law that develops us physically is necessary to our development spiritually. Day after day we can be built up into stronger spiritual beings. We can become more like God, possessing a firmer Christian character and having an integrity that will not swerve for a life nor a world from the path of virtue. Constant progress is constant peace and happiness. It is the triumphant life.

Dear reader, I am going to ask you to lay aside for a few minutes the busy cares of life and come and have a talk with me about spiritual and heavenly things. Now, if you feel that you scarcely have the time, and can not fully dismiss the temporal concerns of life from your mind, then I will excuse you. I do not care to speak with you unless you can give me your undivided attention. I desire to help you if you need help. I want to talk to you about your every-day life, and I do want your calm, serious attention. Surely by God's help we can spend a few minutes to some profit.

Some people hesitate to look closely into their life, lest they find such a delinquency as will disquiet them. Some fear to give a close examination, lest it give Satan an opportunity to accuse them. This need not be. We can look closely into our daily life and not allow Satan to whisper one word to us. We can not make improvement upon our life without close examination in order to discover weakness and imperfections. When we discover them, we must set earnestly to work to correct them. The discovery alone is not sufficient. If we do not correct a fault that we have discovered, we soon lose consciousness of the fault. There are times with every one, no doubt, when it seems that they are making no progress, but these may be the times when we are making most progress.

If we have just one fault, we ought to desire to get rid of it. Our desire should be so great that we shall set about at once to correct that fault. Now, if we say, "Oh, it is such a little thing," then we shall not get free from it, and that little thing may become a greater thing. To be too quick to speak is a fault. The Bible says, "Be slow to speak." If we have the fault of speaking too quickly, we should correct that. We can if we will.

The Bible tells Christians to watch and pray. Christians do not need to watch and pray lest they rob a bank. They would not rob a bank if they never prayed. But we do need to watch arid pray lest we do some little thing that we should not do. I will relate to you the experience of a dear brother who desired to live for God, but who neglected to watch and pray as he should. An evil thought was presented to his mind. Not seeing the evil of it, he indulged the thought, and found pleasure in the indulgence. After a few minutes he felt the reproving of the Spirit of God and so dismissed the thought. Later it came again. It was so pleasing that he indulged it a little longer than before. Again the Spirit reproved him. In a few evenings the thought came again. It was only a little sensual thought, a little imaginary indulgence of the flesh. But it came again and again. It was indulged a little longer and a little longer. Eventually it worked a fleshly lust into his heart, and after two or three years he was led into actual commission of a sinful deed. It was an apparently innocent thought in the beginning, but it ended in sin committed.

There are little yieldings to lightness, impatience, aircastle building, exaggerations, frettings, murmurings, idleness, etc., that prey upon the soul and rob it of peace and the sweet consciousness of God's presence. But there is progress in the divine life for every one of us if we will only give attention to our life as we pass along. The first thing is to have a deep interest in making spiritual gain, and then to be full of faith and encouragement.

Jesus will help you to make some gains each day if you will press your way through the crowd and touch him. It is the earnest prayer of faith that gets us through to God and makes us feel like giants in his strength. If you would be strengthened in your soul, you must exercise. This is the law of development in the spiritual as well as in the animal life. "Exercise thyself unto godliness." This is a motto we should hang upon the walls of our memory. Its meaning is that increase in godliness is attained only by exercise.

I shall have much now to say about your doing, but

bear in mind that the doing is to be not in your strength, but in God's strength. Here are two mottos to keep in remembrance: "Without Him I can do nothing"; "I can do all things through Christ, who strengtheneth me." By the help of the Lord we are going to tell you how to be strong in him. God wants you to be a David. Go out in his strength and meet the Goliaths. They must fall before you. I shall not tell you so much you do not know as I shall endeavor to get you to practise what you know. How many times have you resolved to do and have failed to keep your resolution? Your failure was not because you could not, but because you did not. To make a success in any business enterprise, one must give it constant and daily attention. Likewise, if you make a success in the Christian life, you must give it constant and daily attention. You must make it not only *a* business but *the first* business of your life.

But some make this complaint: "It takes so much time." It will take some time, that is true, and if you do not think you have time, then you had better not begin. What would you think of a man who contemplated engaging in some business, but said he did not have much time to devote to it? You would advise him not to engage in the business at all. It takes time to make advancement in the Christian life. One brother said, "But we must attend to our temporal duties." My reply was, "Shall we not attend to our spiritual duties?" When people talk of having to attend to temporal duties, it appears that they are going to do this if they have to neglect spiritual duties. Unless we have a better enlightenment than this, we shall never make progress in the Christian life.

We have no excuse for not being strong in the Lord.

"Watch ye, stand fast in the faith, quit you like men, be strong." Of course, you need the help of God, but God helps those who help themselves. He will not by some irresistible power convey you to your closet and put you on your knees, but he will give you strength to go if you will use what he gives you.

I will now give you, not learned theology, but plain, simple instruction how to make daily advancement in the divine life and to be strong in God. "Dearly beloved, I beseech you as strangers and pilgrims, abstain from fleshly lusts, which war against the soul." I Pet. 2:11. Any indulgence of the flesh weakens the spiritual powers. The question might arise, "What are fleshly lusts?" We are here in the flesh. The flesh has not only its desires but its needs. To indulge the flesh in its needs is not fleshly lust, but to indulge it in any thing beyond its actual needs is "fleshly lusts." In other words, any intemperance is lust of the flesh. Temperance is a fruit of the Spirit. We are to add temperance to our knowledge. The more knowledge we get of the divine character, the more clearly we can discriminate between fleshly lusts and temperance.

"I keep my body under, and bring it into subjection," says the apostle Paul. He spoke these words when talking about running to obtain an incorruptible crown. He calls our attention to how people run to obtain a corruptible crown, "and every man." he says, "that striveth for the mastery *is temperate in all things*." If men must be temperate in all things in order to obtain a corruptible crown, how much more temperate must we be in order to obtain an incorruptible crown? If the soul does not keep the body under, the body will keep the soul under.

But this keeping under does not consist in many prayers, in long vigils, and fasts, in severe chastenings of the body, in dwelling in a cloister or being a hermit. Do not make this sad mistake. His yoke is easy and his burden is light, yet the Christian life is one of self-denial. But his love in our hearts makes it a delight. We are not to keep our bodies under by prolonged fasts and beatings, but to keep in control the self-seeking that is natural to the self-life of man. The pure in heart have organs of sense, are capable of feeling the impressions made by external objects. It is natural for the individual life of the sanctified to seek ease and comfort. This is not the nature of the divine life in the soul, but is the nature of the self-life of man.

Adam and Eve had this self-life in the purity of their creation; they had organs of sense. It was to these that Satan made his appeals; to the feelings in their self-life, not to the feelings in the divine life of their soul. The will of sense - for such it might be called - overpowered that higher will of the soul, and they yielded to the will of sense as aroused by temptation. We who are pure in heart have this same will of sense. It is this will of sense that must be "kept under." or in control to the will of God. "Not my will [that is, that lower will of my self-life]." said Jesus, "but thy will, be done." I will make this plainer as we go on. I feel like making it as plain and simple as I can, even if doing so does require time, because here lies the secret of success in the Christian life. Those who look upon the instructions herein as trifling will do so to their own spiritual injury.

It is natural for us to avoid hardship and suffering. This is not wrong of itself; it is wrong only when it conflicts with the will of God. It is not wrong for you to avoid burning at the stake unless it be God's will that you should thus end your life. If God wills you to burn at the stake you must not seek to avoid the ordeal. If we do not watch carefully and live close to God and keep our body under, the will of sense will grow strong and cause us to avoid hardships even when God wills us to undergo them. Be careful that you do not mistake the impulse of sense for the divine will. One may say he does not believe it to be God's will that he undergo this suffering when it may be only his own humanity. Out of human sympathy we may try to dissuade our brother from doing the will of God. At Caesarea certain brethren tried, out of mere sympathy, to persuade Paul not to go to Jerusalem, where, it was prophesied, he should be bound and delivered to the Gentiles. Seeing that he would not be persuaded, they gave place to that higher will, and said, "The will of the Lord be done."

This is not confined to the greater affairs of life, such as burning at the stake, but includes the little affairs of every-day life. How easy it is for man to conclude it is the will of God for him to do a certain thing when perhaps it is only the will of sense! Remember, God's ways are not as our ways. It seems to be a most reasonable thing to the minister that he should go home to his family. How easy it is for him to believe it is God's will that he should go! At least, it has been so many times with the writer. He has too often obeyed the human desire and disobeyed God. Such disobedience, if such it may be called, is not sin, since the will of God is not known, but it is being led by the impulse of sense and is detrimental to spirituality. God would have us look more earnestly to him in order to know his will and not yield so readily to mere human desires.

To enjoy nearness to God we must not be influenced by any will of sense. The impulse of sense is so deceptive that, if we are not very watchful and fully surrendered to God with an intense desire to know and do his will, it will prevent our understanding his will to us. It may not be difficult to convince you that it is God's will that your brother should go as a missionary to some foreign field, but very difficult to convince you that it is God's will for you to go, when perhaps it is just as reasonable every way that you should go. It may be the will of sense to remain, that prevents your knowing God's will.

Here is a truth I wish you to think upon: We can not see the folly of any passion clearly when we are strongly tempted by that passion. A sanctified man may eat too much sometimes; he may be intemperate sometimes in the sexual relation; and yet the Word of God says, "Whether ye eat or drink, or whatsoever ye do, do all to the glory of God." Let me say, however, that those who enjoy deep union and communion with God are careful to be temperate in their entire manner of life.

As we have stated before, the pure in heart have organs of sense. These organs can be impressed by external objects. These impressions may properly be termed "feelings." A man filled with the Holy Spirit may, when being praised by some unwise person, be tempted to pride; in other words, he feels a sense of pride. This feeling is in the self-life of the man. A sanctified man is tempted to impatience. He feels a sense of impatience, not carnal, but as an impulse of sense in the self-life. When some one does something contrary to your pleasure or wishes, you may have feelings of displeasure or impatience. The patience of a mother is sometimes tried by the conduct of a child. The trying of patience is simply feelings of impatience in the self-life. But in her patience she is to possess her soul. These feelings of impatience are to be resisted in the strength of the Lord. Resist them with a prayer.

I have now brought you to the place where I am ready to tell you how to grow in grace, how to increase, how to make progress in the divine life, which is all that is meant by the expressions, "getting closer to God," "becoming more like Christ," etc. Remember this: 'feelings are strengthened by being indulged. You are tempted to pride, to lightness, to impatience; you have feelings of pride, lightness, impatience, for this is what temptations are. These feelings should be immediately and indignantly resisted. Get after them in earnest. The very exercise of resisting is what will develop and strengthen the spiritual powers; but if the feelings are indulged, they will grow stronger and the spiritual powers grow weaker. If you value your spiritual prosperity, you will be very quick to resist every temptation. Sometimes people allow a tried, mean, impatient feeling to settle down upon them for hours. They do not feel pleasant, neither do they look pleasant. Such feelings leave their trace behind. They are a dangerous foe. Loathe them, despise them. Go to the Lord in earnest prayer and pray until joy springs up in the soul, a smile beams on the face, and the bad feelings are made to fly away like a startled bird. Some say, "We can not prevent bad feelings and thoughts from attacking us." They use the words of Luther - "We can not prevent birds flying over our heads, but can prevent them from building nests in our hair." It is no sin nor source of discouragement to be attacked by bad feelings and bad thoughts. But bear in mind that we can frighten the birds that are flying over and thus make them fly quickly, and that after being frightened a few times they will fly far around or very high over. So with bad feelings and thoughts: if earnestly and indignantly resisted, they will fly away quickly, and their assaults will grow weaker and weaker. It is God's will that we eat, drink, and sleep; but to be intemperate in these is to destroy spiritual life. We should be guided by a sense of the divine will, and not by a sense of human desire. To yield to the lower will of sense is to be soon abandoned to self and destitute of grace.

I have been asked whether it is possible for us to attain such a degree of perfection that we should never speak a harsh, impatient word or a light word, or be the least intemperate in any way. My answer is that by much prayer, by close watching, and earnest resisting, the will of sense can be so weakened and the soul become so habituated to act under a sense of the divine will that foolish or impatient words, impulsive actions, or any intemperance will be very few and far between. This is being strong in the grace of God.

Again, I have been asked, "Can we reach a place where we shall be no more tempted?" Yes; if you are earnest and faithful, you will reach it when you arrive in that land where flesh and blood can not enter. There you will no more be tempted. But as long as you are here in the flesh, you will be tempted. In the very nature of things you need to be. Your spiritual powers would weaken if they had nothing to resist. Let me here acquaint you with a device of Satan. All these attacks upon the will of sense are made by the devil. He will use some external object to try you. He may withhold temptation for a long time in order that you may become careless and cease to watch and pray, and thus in a measure lose your power of resistance. Then he will come in with a slight attack, so slight you will not detect it in your weakened state. If it be an attack to impatience, you will speak a little hastily, but will scarcely perceive it and will think it of little consequence. But his attacks will grow stronger; your words will grow more hasty; there will be frettings and worryings; and you will be so stupid that you will not be aware of your backsliding. Do not cease your watching and praying even if you have no temptations. Alas, how many have gone down under this cunning device of Satan! This is a scheme he plays well.

When the Christian first starts out on his pilgrimage, he is watchful and prayerful. An attack of Satan startles him, and he becomes earnest in his resistance. If he speaks impatiently or lightly, he flees at once to God for grace, and thus he grows in grace. But if he becomes strong and his soul forms the habit of acting in holiness, he feels strong and ceases his close watching and praying and resisting. Then he slowly but surely retrogrades. Unless he is in some way awakened, he will backslide.

But the question arises, "How can we keep up resistance in order to be strong, if Satan ceases to tempt." Have sham battles. In time of peace soldiers are constantly drilling so that they may be prepared when they come to battle. Pugilists go through much training in preparation for the actual contest. So we are to watch constantly. Keep the soul in a defensive attitude. This is what I mean by sham battles. Bearing in mind that you may be attacked at any time, keep the soul in a defensive attitude; keep up the shield of faith. The very exercise of holding up the shield and keeping the soul in watchings makes it strong for the battle. If you do not exercise your soul in earnest prayer each morning, Satan will likely catch you that day unprepared.

For the perfecting of the soul in the habit of holiness, you must exercise yourself in inward acts of resistance. Keep an intense hatred of sin and the devil; get where you enjoy a contest with Satan; glory in tribulation; rejoice when you are persecuted; count it joy when you are tried and tempted. Soldiers get so they love the battle, pugilists enjoy the contest, and we should be where we love trials. We hate them, therefore we love to conquer them; they afford us means for development, therefore we welcome them; they deepen us into God and make us more like Christ, therefore we hail them with joy. We hate them themselves, but in our intense love for God and the privilege of exercising ourselves in his strength we count all our trials joy. We rejoice in the midst of temptation because we have the opportunity of displaying the strength of our God.

But do not make the mistake of thinking that you are so strong in God that the little evil thought, or the feeling of pride or impatience, or the little act of intemperance, is of no consequence. It is these little things that sap away the spiritual strength. Get after the very least of them and put them to death. Give them no place. If one single word of lightness or of impatience escapes your lips, go in earnest prayer, asking God to make you a conqueror. Seek to have your life wholly free from imperfections, and you will daily advance in the divine life.

  Life is full of peace and pleasure
   When we're saved by grace;
  Sweetest joys overflow the measure
  When we're saved by grace;

Gifts from heaven fall in show'rs,
Cheering dark and lonely hours,
By our pathway bloom sweet flow'rs,
 When we're saved by grace.

E'en in sorrow there are blessings
 When we're saved by grace;
Chastening rods are fond carressings
 When we're saved by grace;
Storm-clouds far away are driven,
Life flows on so sweet and even,
Round us beams the light of heaven,
 When we're saved by grace.

All around is wondrous beauty
 When we're saved by grace;
There is joy in every duty
 When we're saved by grace;
Hope is ever sweetly singing,
Peace-bells in our souls are ringing,
Guardian angels round us winging,
 When we're saved by grace.

We must every day be growing
 When we're saved by grace;
Progress in divine life making,
 When we're saved by grace;
Upward, upward, nearer heaven,
Life more peaceful and more even,
Fuller light upon us beaming,
 When we're growing in grace.

You will, I hope, pardon the writer if he repeats too much. Repetition is sometimes needed that a truth may be enforced. Sometimes line upon line is needful.

What, in its true sense, is a holy life? It is the life of Jesus. His whole manner of life was truly holy. His life is the ideal life. If we would live holy, we must live as he lived. The artist has his ideal before him, and with touches of the brush here and there upon his canvas he forms an exact image of the ideal. The life of Jesus is what we are to imitate. He sets the example of holy living and calls us to the same holy life. "As he which hath called you is holy, so be ye holy in all manner of conversation." I Pet. 1:15. This text has a better rendering in the Revised Version: "Like as he which called you is holy, be ye yourselves also holy in all manner of living." As Christians we are God's offspring, and as such are like him.

Holiness in the life of Jesus is found not only in the great miracles that he performed, but also in the lesser happenings of his life. The restoring of life to the dead is no more beautifully holy than the laying of his hands upon the heads of children and blessing them. His memorable Sermon on the Mount no more portrays the loveliness of his character than does his conversation with the woman by the wayside well. It is the little things in every-day life, if attended to and kept in the meekness and the solemnity of the Spirit of Christ, that make life truly beautiful and holy. It is not the eloquent sermon that makes a life so sublime, but it is the tender smile, the kind word, the gentle look, given to all; it is the patient manner in which all the little trying and provoking things of life are met. You may preach or write ever so forcibly and eloquently, and bring out the sublime truths of the Bible in great beauty; but if in the privacy of your own home there are little frettings, a little peevishness, a little crossness, a little levity, a little selfishness, a little distrust, your life is not as truly holy as it should be.

If you desire God's holy image to be stamped upon your soul, your countenance, and your life, you must carefully avoid the little sprigs of lightness, the little bits of sloth and indolence, touches of forwardness, rudeness, selfishness, etc. Pure words belong to a holy life. You should use the very choicest words, language that is free from vulgarity, slang, and the spirit of the world. Untidiness, uncleanness, carelessness, and shabbiness are not at all beautiful ornaments in a holy life. But quietness, modesty, and reticence are gems that sparkle in a holy life like diamonds set in a band of gold. Give attention to your words, your thoughts, your tone of voice, your feelings; to little acts of benevolence, the practise of self-denial, of promptness, of method and order. These are auxilaries of holy living. Are there not many little things in your home life that you can improve upon? Seek God for help and be truly holy.

LUKEWARMNESS.

A lukewarm life is a displeasure to God; he would have us to be fervent in spirit. God is pleased with us when we are lively stones, but not when we are formal and lukewarm. A lukewarm state is a dangerous state. One very dangerous thing about it is that usually when a person is lukewarm he is unaware that he is lukewarm. If a man is sick and does not know that he is sick, he is in great danger of his life, because he is not at all likely to take the proper care of himself. So the man who is cold and formal but thinks he is spiritual and full of love is not at all likely to do anything for the improvement of his spiritual condition. He is very much like the Irishman's turtle. I hesitate to relate anything so amusing, but it so well illustrates the state of the lukewarm professor that I think I am justifiable.

Some Irishmen had caught a large turtle and cut off his head. Then they waited for him to die, but the turtle scrambled about for some hours. Desiring an explanation of such a phenomenon, they accosted an Irishman who was passing by. After watching the turtle for a moment, he remarked, "He is dead, but he doesn't know it." This is the condition of the lukewarm professors. They are spiritually dead, but are not aware of it. The professors of Christianity at Laodicea were lukewarm, but they thought themselves rich and increased with goods and in need of nothing.

Diseases of the human body are attended with certain feelings and symptoms by which the physician can tell the nature of the affection in a particular case. The diseases of the human soul are also attended with certain symptoms by which the nature of the malady in a given case may be known. I will now tell you of a few of the symptoms of lukewarmness, so you may know whether such is your state.

First. A kind of doubtful or uncertain feeling as to whether you are right with God, together with an unwillingness to examine yourself closely for fear you are wanting. Being filled with the Spirit gives us fulness of assurance.

Second. If when you testify to being saved, sanctified, and ready for the coming of Jesus, your heart fails to say amen and you wish down in your soul you had a little better assurance that what your lips say were true, you are not as spiritual as you should be. When we are filled with the Spirit, our souls are assured and satisfied.

Third. Going along day after day in the same routine of life, taking it for granted that you are at the work the Lord wants you to do, and not earnestly seeking to *know* his will. Those who are spiritual can not be contented without a definite knowledge of the will of God. If you are going along without any real and positive knowledge of the will of God and are not seeking to know it, surely you are lukewarm.

Fourth. If when your routine of life is in some way interrupted, you are dissatisfied and complain; if you do not enjoy being moved out of your old channel, but you wish to be let alone, it is evident that you have chosen your own way and that God is not ordering your steps.

Fifth. If when you are called to the assistance of a neighbor or the sick or even an enemy, you find a reluctancy to go and an often returning of your own mind to your own concerns and a desire to hurry back to them, you are, it appears, looking upon your own things, and not on the things of others. The Bible tells us to look upon the things of others. If you see your own needs, and see and care but little about the things of others, you are selfish. Those who are spiritual have time to help others and do it willingly.

Sixth. If when called upon to go to the assistance of some unfortunate one and you can not possibly go, if you do not have a deep heart-regret and if you do not ofttimes during the day think of the poor unfortunate man and be pained at heart because of your inability to help him, you must be more concerned about yourself than about others. You look on your own things and do not see nor feel the needs of others. If such is true in you, you are in a lukewarm state.

Seventh. If you were to be asked whether you are doing the work you are now doing, solely and purposely for the glory of God, and you should be obliged to answer that you had taken no particular thought about it, but supposed it mattered little to the Lord, just so you were doing something, this would surely show neglect, indifference, lukewarmness.

Eighth. If you are indifferent and unconcerned about making spiritual progress; if you are not desiring and earnestly seeking for more of God; if you are not earnestly striving to be more meek and humble, to be more kind and patient; if you are carelessly tolerating acts of selfishness, of impatience, unkindness, harshness, and lightness, you are certainly lukewarm.

Ninth. Neglect to read the Bible and to pray in secret; greater fervency in public prayer than in secret prayer; more outward manifestation than real inward piety; testifying or preaching beyond the true standard of living - these too are evidences of lukewarmness. A man may become enthusiastic in prayer, testimony, or sermon, and think he is making great advancement; but if he does not live up to every word he speaks, he is losing instead of gaining, because he is not walking in light.

Lukewarmness is very loathsome to God. It reproaches him. To make no profession of love to God at all is not such a reproach to him as to profess love and be lukewarm. God wants all your heart. If he can not have it all, he will have none. He desires warm, fervent love. To love him only partially, and not supremely, makes it appear as if he were worthy of only half-hearted love. It makes other things equal with God.

After the physician learns the symptoms and pronounces the disease, he then prescribes the remedy. Thank God, there is an unfailing remedy for lukewarmness. Of course, "an ounce of prevention is worth a pound of cure." "Repent and do the first works." Come to God and buy of him gold tried in the fire. Exercise yourself in spiritual things if there yet be any love in your heart. Shake off everything that is stupefying. Press your way through to God in spite of dryness and deadness. Stir up your soul. Give yourself to deep meditation upon the great love of God to you. Pray in fervency and faith. Consecrate to the whole will of God. If your case is not hopeless - and it is not - this will effect a cure.

STEADFASTNESS.

"Therefore, my beloved brethren, be ye steadfast, unmovable, always abounding in the work of the Lord." 1 Cor. 15:58. Steadfastness is an essential principle in Christian character. There can be no success nor prosperity in the Christian life when this principle is wanting. The Psalmist said, "My heart is fixed, trusting in the Lord." This is true steadfastness. It is cleaving to God, let the storms rage as they may. It is resting and abiding in Jesus though the trials of life may be the severest possible. It is a firm, fixed, settled decision to abide in doctrines of the Bible. It is to rest confidingly upon the teaching and promises of the Holy Scriptures. Just as a man lies confidently down to rest upon his bed, so a Christian, in his steadfastness, rests confidingly, rests without fear, upon the never-changing Word of God.

Through Jesus Christ, Christians are made partakers of the divine nature. They receive the imprint of divine character in their souls. Among the different principles in the character of God is found steadfastness. When God delivered Daniel from the lions, Darius the king said, "I make a decree that in every dominion of my kingdom men tremble and fear before the God of Daniel: for he is the living God, and steadfast forever." Dan. 6:26. Just as Christian fortitude is noble, manly, and pleasing to God, so a lack of steadfastness is ignoble, unmanly, and highly displeasing to God.

Some (it may be many) are led by their feelings. We, as the children of God, are to be led by the Spirit of God; but not all fully understand what is meant by "being led by the Spirit." I would rather be led by a sense of duty than by my feelings. I do not understand that in order to be led by the Spirit we need always to have a strong inward impression or almost audible voice speaking to us. The Spirit of God has illuminated the Word and enlightened your mind to know what is your Christian duty; hence when you go forward and discharge your duties faithfully, you are truly being led by the Spirit. You know it to be your duty to help the poor, to support the weak, to comfort the sorrowful, to attend religious services, to witness for Jesus, to study the Scriptures, to pray, and diligently to follow every good work. You may sometimes feel a strong impression to pray, but you do not need to have this feeling always in order to be duty-bound to pray. It is your duty to pray, to give of your means, etc., oftentimes just as much when you do not feel impressed to do so as when you have strong inward impressions. You do not need to wait for such impressions before you act, for a knowledge of your duty makes you responsible.

A man can have no true steadfastness who is influenced by his emotions or impressions. The man who is steadfast, unmovable in the Word, goes forward to a discharge of his known duties, no matter what his feelings may be. Whatever may be his impressions to do a certain thing, if it is not consistent with the Word and the Spirit and his knowledge of right, he persistently refuses to obey.

How the true principle of steadfastness abides in the will of God and the doctrines of Christ is demonstrated in the teachings of Barnabas to the church at Antioch. There was some contention in the church over circumcision, and heavy persecutions from without, and many were being moved from the true faith. Barnabas exhorted that with purpose of heart they cleave to the Lord. Steadfastness is a firm, fixed purpose of the heart to cleave unto God, to attend strictly and promptly to every Christian duty. It is a decided, unchangeable, unshaken purpose of the heart to obey implicitly the teachings of the Savior, regardless of the feelings.

You will find that, if you attend to every Christian duty, you will often have to go contrary to your feelings. How often the enemy of your soul will, if he can, cast indifferent feelings over you concerning prayer. That is the time to show your Christian fortitude and steadfastness. It is weakness and laziness to neglect prayer simply because we do not feel inclined to pray. To yield to indifferent feelings is to encourage them, and they will grow stronger and stronger, so that we shall feel less and less inclined to pray. The more we pray, the more prayerful we feel; likewise, the less we pray, the less prayerful we feel. When we have yielded to indifferent feelings for sometime and have sadly neglected prayer, we have a hard struggle to get through to the glorious light and victory and sweetness. But you must get out where the blessings fall; you must get where you have sweet tastes of love and the satisfying blessings of the presence of God. You must be courageous, manly, and decided. The way to enjoy serving God and doing our full Christian duty is always to do our duty and especially at those times when doing it seems to be the least enjoyable.

Steadfastly resist Satan and every indifferent feeling, and do your duty at any cost. Remember, it is not he that feels to do good and doeth it not, but "he that knoweth to do good and doeth it not, to him it is sin,"

HOW TO UNDERSTAND GOD'S WILL.

In order to do God's will we must first know his will. In order to have real satisfaction, rest, and contentment in the Christian life - and there is no true rest outside the Christian life - we must have the full assurance that we are doing the will of God. The soul that loves God can not be satisfied with anything less than this. As long as there is a doubt, there can not be perfect contentment. We must have a perfect knowledge of God's will concerning us, or else we shall not fully know we are doing his will.

Many are saying, "I would gladly do God's will if I only knew what was his will." Such ones have not reached that nearness to God that they should. There should always be a clear and definite understanding between God and his children. "My sheep," Jesus says, "hear my voice"; and we know that God hears the voice of his children. We can talk to God and God to us; consequently, there can be understanding between us. You can live close enough to God to know his will - not merely to suppose his will or take it for granted, but to know it because he told you. A man's employees may suppose they are doing what he wants them to do, but this does not give them full assurance. It is only when they have been in his presence and heard him express his will that they know they are doing it. You can know God's will. You need not spend one day without knowing you are in his order.

The Scripture says, "Wherefore be ye not unwise, but understanding what the will of the Lord is." Eph. 5: 17. In the verses preceding this one we are told to walk circumspectly and to redeem the time. We need to know God's will that we may use every opportunity to the greatest advantage. To pass along day after day without a definite knowledge of being in the will of God or without taking much thought about it or earnestly seeking to know it, is living on entirely too low a spiritual plane. God wants you to come up higher - high enough and close enough to know his will. Has not God purchased you? You are his servant, his bondslave. You are to do everything you do for him. He who has men in his employ expects them to do his will. They do not go out a single day ignorant of his will. They do not always wait to be told what to do, but they make inquiry. With many there may not be enough earnest seeking after God to know his will.

In order to know God's will there must be a perfect consecration to God. The soul must lay down her own will and present herself before God as much as to say, "I give up my way and will forever to be thine and thine alone; to love thee and serve thee; to do thy whole will now and forever." There must be humility before God; a deep inner consciousness of your nothingness and your inability to accomplish anything in life of yourself. "The meek he will guide in judgment." We must be meek and humble before the Lord and confess that we are dependent on him and that life will be an utter failure unless he wills and guides and plans and works in us and with us and for us.

There must be great love to God and an earnest desire

to know his will. Without strong desire to know God's will you can never learn it. It is those who desire that obtain answers to their prayers; and that desire must be really great. You must seek to know. Where there is great desire, there will be earnest seeking; but there will not be earnest seeking without the fervent desire. The desire must be so intense that you feel as if you must know. You must feel that you can not get along in life without knowing God's will. You can not be of any service to him without having knowledge of his will. You must also have faith. When you ask God to teach you his will, you must believe he will do it, and he will do it. When he begins to unfold his will, you must move in his order without doubting or questioning. He will guide you and direct your every step, and you can know that you are doing the very thing God wants you to do. Bless his name! Such a life is heaven here.

A VIEW OF JESUS.

Let us take a look at Jesus. Let us pray that the Holy Spirit may unveil him and present him to us clearly. Now we see him. We see him as our all and as in all. Can you see him thus? Is he everything to you? and is he in everything that comes to you?

Let us take a view of Jesus through two texts of Scripture. First, "And hath put all things under his feet." Eph. 1:22. We see him as our protector. Christ has conquered all, and God has put all things under his Son's feet. In all the world there is no evil thing that can harm the child of God. Jesus cares for his children. How safe we feel! He is our refuge, our strong tower, our buckler, and our shield. Discouragements, doubts, fears, disease, Satan, and all that would antagonize us are under his feet and so can never do us harm.

Second, "The Father loveth the Son, and hath given all things into his hand." Every good thing is in the hand of Jesus. He stands ready to give them to his children. There is not a need you can ever have but Jesus has in his hand something with which to supply that need. His loving hand is extended to you. It contains something that will meet all your needs in life. Praise the Lord!

Nothing can harm us, for every harmful and harming

thing is beneath the feet of our Lord. So we need not fear. We can never fail to have all our needs supplied, for Jesus stands with outstretched hand to give just what we need just when we need it. Do you see Jesus as such? Open your eyes wide, look and live, and be happy and free.

DEVOTION TO GOD.

Devotion to God implies ardent affection for him - a yielding of the heart to him with reverence, faith, and piety in every act, particularly in prayer and meditation. We catch a glimpse of the true meaning of devotion from what is said of the centurion of the Italian band. He was termed a devout man because he feared God, gave much alms to the people, and prayed to God always (see Acts 10:2). This is the essence of true devotion. He loved God, without which there can be no devotion. The more we love an object, the more devoted to it we are. Devotion is therefore love manifested. At the feet of Jesus stood a woman weeping and washing his feet with her tears and wiping them with the hairs of her head and kissing them. Is not this a picture of devotion? It is love and devotion expressed in action. Jesus said, "She loved much." The secret of devotion is loving *much*.

Every devoted Christian desires to be more devoted to his God. I am glad we can be. It is pleasant to feel in our hearts an ardent desire to love God more. A fond mother clasps her babe to her bosom. She loves it, and her heart is happy in that love; but she feels she can not love it enough. She longs to love it more. Her heart yearns to love it more, though she loves it from the fulness of her soul. This longing to love increases our capacity to love. By being filled with air some vessels are made to expand. Unless filled to their utmost capacity, they would not become more extended. To the extent that the heart is filled with the love of God, man is happy.

To desire to be more devotional is not an evidence of lack of devotion, but, on the contrary, an evidence of devotion. Those who are the least devotional have the least desire to be more devotional. The heart that is fullest of love is happiest; and although it is happy and satisfied, yet it longs to move. Oh, how we long to clasp our arms more tightly about him! how we long to have him clasp his arms more tightly about us! how we long to nestle more fondly and lovingly on his bosom! What rapture to our love-flooded souls to receive of his caresses and hear his tender words! To the soul in the ecstasy of its heavenly love, the world with its pleasures has vanished away like a morning vapor.

It is not understood by all how and why we should have a desire to possess more of that of which we are already full. It is the desire for development; it is an innate desire; it is a principle planted in our constitution under grace. Let me repeat what I have said elsewhere: Every living thing consciously or unconsciously struggles to conform to type. When the little plant bursts through the ground, it enters the race in conforming to the type that it carries in its bosom. Thus, in the heart of the acorn is a miniature oak-tree. The little chick carries within it an image of the mother bird, to which it will naturally though unconsciously conform.

In the natural world when things reach the highest point of development, they begin to decay or deteriorate; but this is not true in the spiritual world.

Never in this life and possibly never in that life which is to come shall we reach the fulness of the type, or, in other words, the highest point of development. As the acorn or the little chick bears in its nature an image of the parent, so the Christian bears in his soul the image of God. This is the image to which he is to conform. Day after day he can grow in grace. Day after day the beautiful graces of the Spirit can become more beautiful and the exterior life be more perceptibly stamped with the holy image of God. There must be progress, or there will be regress. When a ball that has been thrown upward ceases to ascend, it begins to descend. When the fulness of the type is reached, then begins the retrogression. This is none the less true of spiritual things. The reason why there need be no declension in love is because the highest point of development is never attained.

For illustration let us set a little child in our midst. As a child it is perfect. All its organs are in proper place and are properly performing their functions. It is a perfect image of the type of man into which it will grow. That child's nature tends toward, and the child longs to be, a man. The child's innate desire for development does not make it discontented as long as its craving for growth is gratified. In this we behold the goodness and the wisdom of the Creator. That the child may be happy, it is so constituted that it satisfactorily meets all the requirements of the law of development. The child is thus kept in a state of contentment. Did it seek to fulfil the law of growth contrary to its nature, to become a man would be an irksome task. It is a delight to the child to eat, to play, to sleep. And these things, producing growth, meet the demands of its nature. There is implanted in it both a desire to grow and a relish for the things necessary to its growth. Thus the entire process of development is a delight. In fact, there will be no delight or enjoyment unless there be development.

True, a child does not eat and play for the express purpose of growing. Indeed, it may take no thought about growing. But there is in the nature of the child, when in health, a demand for growth. When the child is in ill health, the growth ceases; consequently there is no demand for development, and it loses relish for the things that go to meet that demand.

This very beautifully illustrates Christian development which includes becoming more devotional. You desire to be more devotional. Such a desire is legitimate. The nature of every sanctified soul craves development. The soul is not dissatisfied, any more than the growing child. As that developing life in the child moves it to seek for the things that produce development, so the life of God in the sanctified soul moves it to seek for the things that will unfold and amplify that life. "If ye be risen [have life] with Christ, seek those things which are above." Those things, coming into our soul daily, will unfold us more and more into an heavenly life. They are food to the sanctified soul. They keep the soul satisfied, because they are the means provided by a loving, all-wise Providence for the constant healthful growth of our spiritual natures. Herein only is true soul-rest.

God gives us a relish for the very things that go to fulfil the demands of our Christian nature. Prayer, meditation, reading the Bible, trust, and resting in the Lord promote increase in him. How delightful is prayer to the soul that is healthful and growing! and the Word of God is sweeter than honey. Where there is a demand in the soul for these things, how delightful it is to engage in them! Do you behold the beauty and the wisdom here? God implants a desire in the soul for spiritual development and at the same time implants a relish for the things necessary for such development. Bless his name! Understand me, please, this desire is not a restless longing, an aching void, as is found in an unregenerate heart or in a soul in spiritual decline; but it is the delightful struggling of a soul bearing the likeness of God, to conform to the natural law of development pent up within its bosom.

What is it in the nature of the oak that causes it to send its root down into the soil and to drink up of its substance? What is it in the nature of the child that causes it so eagerly to eat and play? It is the demand in their nature for growth, or that innate struggle to conform to type. Manhood is sleeping in the child's bosom, and it wrestles and struggles to rise to the fulness of that image. What causes the Christian heart to long to root deeper into God; that makes the soul seek his embrace? It is that instinctive struggle to conform to God's glorious image. The entire process of development is delightful. Whenever the natural tendency toward growth ceases, the soul is in an abnormal state, and loses relish for the things necessary to growth.

Christian, see to it that you keep in your heart a desire, a longing, a panting, or, if you would rather I will say, a demand, in your spiritual being to be more devotional to God, and meet that demand by resting by faith in him, by prayer, by meditation, by service. Do this, and you will become more devotional. But I love the word "desire." Desire in the soul for spiritual things is appetite. Satisfying this desire is a pleasure. Never were any viands so sweet to the physical sense of taste as that food to our soul which helps us be more devotional. "Desire" is a Bible term. "As new-born babes, *desire* the sincere milk of the word, that ye may grow thereby."

Before concluding this chapter I will call your attention to one way of becoming more devotional - being active in service. Desire must be gratified, or it will die. Likewise, motive must find expression in action, or it will die. You have a desire for prayer; then grant that desire by actually praying, or you will lose the desire. An appetite once lost is difficult to regain. You may have in your soul a pure motive; then carry it into action. Do something for God, and you will become more devotional to God. Not that devotion comes by works, to begin with, any more than grace; but we do become more devotional by doing, just as we grow stronger physically by exercise. Follow out every inclination to do good as far as you can, and you will become more devotional to your God.

God loves to have you devoted to him, and he longs to have you more devoted. It is astonishing, nevertheless God has intense desire to be prayed to and great love for communion with our hearts. He says, "My son, give me thine heart." What does he want with man's heart? He wants to put his love in it, so he can be loved by it and hold communion with it. "The prayer of the upright is his delight." Oh, that there are so few hearts that love God! Jesus wept over Jerusalem because they would not come to him. But why does he so intensely yearn for the prayers and devotions of our hearts? Because it is another young life struggling to conform to the image in which it was created. It is another soul which has been won for God and in which he has his throne.

O God! take our hearts and compress within them that pure love from thy own heart that will cause us to pray, "O God! enlarge our hearts." God would even pain our hearts with the fulness of his love until we find no ease except in expansion.

THE GOLDEN RULE OF LIFE.

"And as ye would that men should do to you, do ye also to them like wise." Luke 6:31. This is a good rule for every-day living. It is known throughout the Christian world as "The Golden Rule." It has great depths. It contains more no doubt than any of us comprehend. But let us study it for a moment. We might divide it into two rules: First, Do good to all; second, Do harm to none. We would that all men should do us good, and we would that none should do us harm. But if we would see the greater depths of this rule, we must look beyond the physical man. To do good to all and harm to none in a bodily or physical sense is indeed good, but to do good to all and harm to none in a moral sense is much better. We should do all we can to help others in a moral sense. Is not this what we would have all men do to us? We should do harm to none in a moral sense, because we would have none do us harm. This necessitates living a very holy life.

There are two ways in which we may do good to men morally: first, by strengthening the good that is in them; second, by suppressing and helping them to overcome any evil or fault that may be in them. Likewise, there are two ways in which we may do harm to men morally: first, by strengthening and encouraging the evil and fault that may be in them; second, by suppressing and destroying the good that may be in them.

We are all creatures of influence. We are being influenced, and we are having an influence. There never was a human life but that had some influence over some other human life. We influence more by example than by words. If we say one thing and act another, we shall find our actions speaking more loudly than our words. If we love God with all our hearts, that love will influence another to love him. Never was love lost. The love you have, O child of God, will find its way into some other life sometime, somewhere. The more of God's love is beaming out of our heart and life, the greater will be our influence upon others. Then may we love him with all the heart. We should be filled with the Spirit. If we are spiritual, we cause those we converse with to desire to be more spiritual. We should be full of faith that our strong faith may help others to have more faith. We should like for others to be such an example to us; and as we would that men should do to us, let us do to them.

It is a very great source of regret, indeed, to be so destitute of love, faith, and spirituality that we discourage and dampen the ardor of those into whose presence we may be for a time. Be your very best for God every day of your life and wield a holy influence over the hearts of men. The very greatest benefit we can be to man and the highest homage we can pay to God is to be filled with all the fulness of God.

TIMELINESS IN DOING GOOD.

To spend well this one brief life of ours, we must be active in doing good. This we have already learned. But not only should we be active in doing good, but we should do the good act when the act will be most helpful. Do the good deed when the good deed needs to be done. The kind word may be worth much and be greatly helpful to the fainting soul today, but may be too late tomorrow. "As we have therefore opportunity, let us do good unto all men." Will you stop a moment and think over these words? Let no opportunity of doing good go by you unimproved. To neglect the present opportunity of doing good and then never be able to do it is a sad thing.

"Of all sad words of tongue or pen
The saddest are these: 'It might have been.'"

Why do you keep all the kind thoughts and kind words for a man until he is dead? They do him no good then. It is while he is living that he needs them. He has burdens heavy to be borne; troubles gather thick over his head; he is neglected and even misrepresented. You can help him with a smile or a few kind words; but, no, you pass him by. Now he is brought to the grave. As the cold clods fall upon his plain coffin, you say, "Well, he was a good man, after all." Why did you not tell him that when he was living? It would have buoyed up his spirit then; it would have made him feel that life was not all in vain and that yet he might do a little good. But now he hears not your words. They return to you or float out into empty space a mere sound. The ear that was once eager for them and the heart that was aching for them is now cold in death. Your kind, cheering words are too late to give him encouragement; your flowers are too late to be appreciated. Once they would have brightened his life, but now his life is over. Once you could have chased away some clouds that were darkening his life, but you did not, and that day has gone into eternity as a day of darkness. You might have brightened it. This morning some kind hand placed a vase of beautiful flowers upon my desk. As I write, their fragrance reaches me and brings me tidings of some one's kind remembrance.

It costs but little to speak kind words, but oh! ofttimes they are worth so much! I know of nothing that costs so little to give that is so valuable to receive. But why keep all the flowers, the kind words, the tender feelings and thoughts, and the sympathetic tears until the one to whom they should be given passes away, and then come and let them fall so gently upon the casket? Do you know of one who is weary? do you know of one who is being misrepresented? do you know of one who is being trodden down by others, with scarcely any one to speak a word of comfort? Now, what would Jesus do? Look at poor Lazarus - turned away by the rich, neglected and rejected; watched over by angels ready to gather him to paradise when he passes beyond the need of aid from men. Why not be an angel and make a day of paradise for him here? Let us do some angel-work while here in life. The angels are ministering spirits. They whisper, "Be of good cheer," "Peace on earth." They come to gladden hearts; they come to close the lions' mouths; they come to open the prison doors and break the iron bands. Oh, let us do some angel-work!

Hast thou any flowers for me?
Wilt thou kindly let them be
Given ere death be-dews my brow?
Wait not, give them to me now.

While in life's eventful day
Tried, and weary grows the way,
When in dark and lonely hour,
Give me then the cheering flow'r.

Hast thou kind words to impart,
Words that lift the fainting heart?
Speak ere Death's hand on me lay;
Speak those kind words now - today.

Kind words are but empty breath
To the heart that's still in death;
When life's load is hard to bear
Let me then the kind word hear.

Hast thou sunlit smiles to give,
Smiles that make us want to live?
Ere I cross death's sullen stream,
On me let those bright smiles beam.

Smiles, whate'er their power to save,
Can not penetrate the grave.
Ere I reach life's ending mile,
Give to me the sunlit smile.

Prayer can stay the trembling knee:

If thou hast but one for me,
Let it offered be today,
Ere the life-light fades away.

When my soul transcends the air,
I no more shall need thy prayer:
Let now, today, thy soul travail;
'Tis only now thy prayers avail.

"If I should die tonight,
My friends would call to mind with loving thought
Some kindly deed the icy hand had wrought,
Some gentle word the frozen lips had said,
Errands on which the willing feet had sped;
The memory of my selfishness and pride,
My hasty words, would all be put aside,
And so I should be loved and mourned tonight."

THE WARFARE OF A CHRISTIAN LIFE.

It is blessed and glorious to be a Christian. No other life is so beautiful and pure; no other life is so tranquilly peaceful; no other is so full of rest, happiness, and satisfaction. The Christian, however, does not go to heaven on flowery beds of ease. His pathway is not strewn with roses all the way; there is now and then a thorn. It is not sunshine all the time; now and then a shadow falls. To win heaven he must fight. There are some things to oppose a Christian on his pilgrimage to the skies; these he must contend against. The contending against those things prepares him for his blissful home above.

"All things work together for good to them that love God." Heaven's blessings and hell's venom, angels' smiles and Satan's frowns, comforts of grace and spiritual wickedness, good and ill, love and hatred, all work good to those who have union with God. It is the battle that disciplines and makes strong and brave the warrior, and not the victory. We are exhorted to "endure hardness as a good soldier." There are some things to endure along the Christian way. James says, "Blessed is the man that endureth temptation." Temptations are outward influences acting upon our natural emotions and passions to induce the will to act contrary to the law of grace to satisfy self. We need not expect to be free from temptations; therefore let us settle it that we will endure them. It is really a blessed thing to endure them. You may think it would be a blessed thing to be free from them, but such would not be the case. It is more blessed to endure them. Temptations will never cease to attack the soul as long as it inhabits this "muddy vesture of decay." Be brave, O soul, and endure temptations. Be brave and fight the good fight of faith. Do not faint because you have temptations. Do not fear because there are long and fierce battles to fight. Be strong and of good courage. It is a life-long struggle, and it is also a life-long victory, and in the end eternal victory. Strong and well-developed spiritual sinews are the result of resisted temptations.

It is not sinful to be tempted. We never lose any spirituality by being tempted. It is the slight yieldings that cause a leaking, a loss of grace. Clear up the vision of your faith a little and take a look at your beautiful glittering crown of life. It is not gold, neither crystal. Do not look at it as such, but see it a crown of life. Yes, you will be crowned with eternal life if you will but endure temptation. Think of this in the hour of thy sore trial. Fight on; heaven awaits to reward you.

LIVE BY FAITH.

Live by faith. There is no other true and right way to live. Without faith it is impossible to please God, and of course the life that pleases God is the only life that is perfect. We can please God; we can walk each day in a way that is pleasing to him. Such a walk is by faith, not by sight. God honors faith. He loves to have his Word believed. He delights to hear the prayer of faith; it avails with him.

Around the great white throne in heaven the angels are shouting day and night, "Holy, holy, holy, Lord God Almighty! blessing and glory and wisdom and thanksgiving, honor and power, belong to thee." But amid all this sound of praise God hears a voice and bends an ear to listen. It is the prayer of faith from the heart of one of his children. There is never too many angels singing nor too many harps resounding for God to hear the voice of his child. "My voice," said the sweet singer of Israel, "shalt thou hear in the morning." He hears the first faint cry of his heaven-born child. Even the unuttered wish of the heart, the unexpressed desire, the faintest breathing of love, he hears and recognizes as the voice of his child. Faith will wing its way into the presence of God. It traverses the universe until it finds him and there brings the soul to its rest. Faith will guide us through this world.

Faith touches God. A woman came to Jesus and tremblingly reached out her feeble hand and touched the hem of his garment. He asked, "Who touched me?" It was not the finger-touch that he felt, but the faith-touch. Today we can touch him by faith and by no other way. Though many angels may be thronging him, yet the feeblest touch of faith will reach him. You may be one of the weakest ones, unnoticed and unknown. A little cabin on the mountainside may be your home, but your feeblest cry of faith will reach the throne of God, and he will send angels to encamp round about you and deliver you. *Have faith in God.* When all is dark around you, believe in him. Trust him when you can not trace, and believe when you can not see. Never doubt his Word. Faith will prevail and bring you the desire of your heart. Will you believe?

A VALUABLE LEGACY.

A legacy is a gift that some one makes to another; usually something that one leaves behind, when departing from this world, for others to enjoy. Some have left great sums of money to others and to institutions, and these bequests have been called valuable legacies. I am now to tell you of the greatest and most valuable legacy that has ever been left to man. It is a bequest left not to one man but to all men. It is not a legacy of silver or gold or diamonds nor of houses and lands. Nor can this precious gift be purchased with gold. It is something Jesus gives; and what he has can not be purchased with any earthly thing. I will read you what it is: "Peace I leave with you, my peace I give unto you." These are the words that Jesus uttered just before his departure from the world, and this is the legacy he leaves to man. Oh, what a gift! We can all possess it. We need it as we are crossing the sea of life. Many storms arise and billows roll high, but the soul possesses this valuable treasure of peace. There is a stillness, a calmness, a peacefulness, in the soul that stormy winds can never disturb.

This peace that Jesus gives, is given us through our obedience. "Oh, that thou hadst hearkened to my commandments! then had thy peace been as a river." What is more peaceful than the calm, even flowing of a river? As we look upon it a quiet peacefulness begins to spread its mantle over our hearts. Still waters are a beautiful emblem of peace, while troubled waters are a picture of unrest.

This peace that Jesus gives is unlike anything that the world gives. This world contains many pleasant things and makes many very liberal offers, but peace is never found by accepting any of them. The pleasures of this world leave a bitter taste, while the hardships we endure for Jesus sweetens our cup.

Shall we analyze this peace, that we may know all about it, even the very hidden secret of the principle? The apostle says, "The peace of God, which *passeth all understanding*, shall keep your hearts and minds." Let us be satisfied to have our hearts and minds kept by this wonderful peace, though we do not understand it. I have some flowers on my desk. There are white ones and yellow and purple and red and pale blue. I do not understand the principle of life that gives them such beauty and fragrance. If I should dissect them in order to discover this secret, I should destroy their beauty and be no wiser. We can not understand this peace, but we can possess it.

There is power in this peace to keep the heart and mind. "Let the peace of God rule in your hearts." Give thy heart over to its calm, still power. It will rule very quietly in your soul, but rule with kingly power. The waters can not rise in trouble where peace holds sway. When this secret power has dominion in our hearts, it speaks peace to all around. It says to the waves and the winds, "Peace, be still." On the attacking fears, on the threatening circumstances, it lays a quiet hand and whispers, "Peace, be still," and great is the calmness of thy soul.

SOME SCRIPTURES FOR DAILY PRACTISE.

If we seek God earnestly in the prayer of faith to help us in our daily practise of the following Scriptural texts and then put forth our best efforts, we shall find life daily growing more holy and beautiful. The beauty and enjoyment of a holy life is that it can always be improved upon. We can live in all the light that shines upon us from these texts today, but tomorrow we find them shining a little brighter and fuller light, so that we shall have to live a little more holy than we are living today. Thus, all along our Christian way we shall find that we are growing and becoming holier in life, and more of the transcendent beauty of Jesus will be seen upon us.

"And be ye kind one to another, tender-hearted, forgiving one another, even as God for Christ's sake hath forgiven you." Eph. 4:32. Let this law of kindness get into your life as its very essence. It is not enough to affect kindness; we must be kind. A tender heart is the groundwork of kindness. Out of such a soil the beautiful flowers of gentleness, kindness, and tenderness grow. These perfume the life and make it cheering to others. Can you be more kind in your daily life? Is your heart so tender that it feels the suffering of the child or the pain of the dumb animal to the extent that you find pleasure in giving relief even at the expense of self-ease?

"Set your affection on things above, not on things on the earth." Col. 3:2. Guard your heart. "Keep it with all diligence." See that all of its affections are on things above. Some of the earthly things that God has given into your keeping will want some of your affection. The beautiful home, the farm, the bank-account, the domestic animals, and even some things almost worthless will want a little of your heart's love. Your own talents and personal appearance may desire some of your affection, just enough to set you approving them for your own sake. Practise daily the above text.

"In everything give thanks." 1 Thess. 5:18. "Giving thanks always for all things." Eph. 5:20. Thankfulness is a grace easily improved and developed if cultivated. Likewise, it will very soon degenerate if neglected. In order to keep a deep sense of thankfulness in our hearts, we must be mindful of the gracious dealings of God. It is well to take time as often as circumstances will permit to meditate in some quiet place upon the goodness of God to you. We should have such thankful hearts that ofttimes tears of gratitude will flow at the remembrance af God's goodness.

"Rejoice evermore." 1 Thess. 5:16. "As sorrowful, yet alway rejoicing." 2 Cor. 6:10. "Rejoice alway: and again I say, Rejoice." Phil. 4:4. "Count it all joy when ye fall into divers temptations." Jas. 1:2. This is the power of the Christian life. We can always rejoice. We can be contented and happy, whatever our circumstances in life. God's grace will sustain us. Every day can be, and should be, a day of rejoicing. God is pleased to have us happy, but he would have our rejoicing to be in him and not in his blessings. To rejoice in the midst of trial is health to the soul.

"Pray without ceasing." 1 Thess. 5:17. "Continue in prayer, and watch in the same with thanksgiving." Col. 4:2. "Praying always with all prayer and supplication in the Spirit, and watching thereunto with all perseverance and supplication for all saints." Eph. 6:18. If you value peace and prosperity of soul, you will not neglect to pray. It is prayer that keeps us up above the clouds and brings heaven down. He who does not pray at all is not a Christian, and he who does not pray much is not much of a Christian. It is not those who have plenty of time to pray that do the most praying, but they who take the time. Let there be some prayer every day.

"Let nothing be done through strife or vainglory; but in lowliness of mind let each esteem others better than themselves." Phil. 2:3. This should be the experience of your heart every day. When we are lowly, we see our own faults and imperfections and our brother's virtues; therefore we look upon him as better than ourselves. It seems to us that others are more humble than we are, and have more faith and love God more than we do.

"Look not every man on his own things, but every man also on the things of others." Phil. 2:4. We should be as much concerned in others' welfare as in our own. He who is looking out for himself and neglecting others has not advanced very far in the Christian life. The Christian lives for others. He will overlook his own needs and see his brother's needs.

"See that none render evil for evil unto any man; but ever follow that which is good, both among yourselves, and to all men." I Thess. 5: 15. "And let us not be weary in well-doing: for in due season we shall reap, if we faint not. As we have therefore opportunity, let us do good unto all men, especially unto them who are of the household of faith." Gal. 6:9, 10. To go about doing good out of a heart full of love is the way to spend life. Heaven is going to reward us according to our works. The Bible tells us so. Never a day should go by without our having done some good thing purposely out of love to God and man. The Lord does not overlook small deeds when done in love. A coral is very small, but many of them make an island: a little good deed done every day will in a lifetime amount to enough to build a splendid mansion in heaven.

"Bear ye one another's burdens, and so fulfil the law of Christ." Gal. 6:2. To lift a load from off the shoulders of another is noble service. To remove a burden from another's heart is truly Christlike. He who goes through life bearing the burdens of others has found the easiest road; he who goes through life refusing to aid others travels a road of hardest toil.

"Abhor that which is evil." Rom. 12:9. God is holy; consequently he hates that which is evil. When we admire the holiness of God, we loathe sin; if sin has no horror to our soul, holiness has no beauty. To the extent we love holiness, to that extent we hate sin. A good man of long ago said, "If I could see the shame of sin on the one hand and the pain of hell on the other, and must of necessity choose one, I would rather be thrust into hell without sin than go to heaven with sin."

Sin is a hideous monster. Draw near to God if you would see sin's awful hideousness. Unlike most other things, the farther you are away from sin the more clearly you can see it as it really is.

"Cleave to that which is good." Rom. 12:9. To cleave to is to adhere tightly; to cling. We cleave to that which is good by ever doing good. When we hate sin as we should and see its awful shame, and love the good and see its wondrous beauty, we would rather go to hell doing good than to heaven committing sin.

"Draw nigh to God." Jas. 4:8. The close of every day should find us a little nearer God than the evening before. We should hide a little more secretely in his pavilion. We should nestle a little more closely under his wing; his feathers should cover us a little more fully. Be the storms what they may, we can daily live very close to God, and what we can do it is our duty to do.

"Open thy mouth wide." Psa. 81:10. We should daily live with wide-open mouth. If we will, the promise is that God will fill it. For God to be all to us, we must expect all from him. God can impart to us only what our hearts are open to receive. If we would live with God in our own soul, we must have all our soul open to receive him. Many fail to see the beauty of a life hid with God because they are looking too much earthward. Opening the mouth wide implies an abandonment of ourself to God with a readiness to receive all that God has to give, together with an expectation to receive nothing that does not come from him. Then God will fill us daily with himself. There will be a constant inflowing from God of strength and ability to perform every duty of life, and of grace and peace to make life an emblem of heaven. "The God of our fathers hath chosen thee, that thou shouldest *know* his will." Acts 22:14. "Not with eye-service, as menpleasers; but as the servants of Christ, *doing* the will of God from the heart." Eph. 6:6. "I *delight* to do thy will,

O my God" Psa. 40:8. It is our privilege to daily *know* the will of God. It is our duty to daily *do* it. It is a blessing to love to do it. Here is the sum of all Christian living: 1. Knowing the will of God; 2. Doing the will of God; 3. Doing the will of God in love.

"I asked the New-year for some motto sweet,
Some rule of life with which to guide my feet;
I asked, and paused; he answered soft and low,
'God's will to know.'

"'Will knowledge then suffice, New-year?' I cried,
And e'en the question into silence died:
The answer came, 'Nay, but remember, too,
God's will to do.'

"Once more I asked: 'Is there no more to tell?'
And once again the answer sweetly fell,
'Yes, this one thing all other things above:
God's will to love.'"

"Do all things without murmurings and disputings." Phil. 2:14. Let thy life be free from all frettings and worryings. Let it be like the calm flowing of the river. God is a strong and high tower, a refuge, a shield. With our life hidden in him, worries and frettings can not reach us. We may be treated unjustly by a bosom friend, but we commit it to God, and instead of feeling the wound the friend gives, we feel the balm our Father gives.

"Be content with such things as ye have." Heb. 13:5. "I have learned, in whatsoever state I am, therewith to be content." Phil. 4:11. He who has gained contentment has gained more than he who has gained the wealth of a world, if it be contentment with godliness. A discontented life is a dark spot on the page of human history. An even, contented life is as a lighthouse shedding its peaceful beams over the turbulent waters where voyagers come and go.

"I can do all things through Christ which strengtheneth me." Phil. 4:13. "I am mighty enough for all things through Christ who empowers me." - Rotherham. There is no excuse for your not living a perfectly victorious life today. You can be a conqueror. Temptations will assail you, trials will come, but you can ignore them in such a way as to show their author your contempt for both him and his temptations. I read just this morning this good suggestion: "Do not dwell upon your temptations. They are like little dogs that bark after a man that passes by; if he stops to drive them away, they bark more fiercely than before." You can do all things through Christ, but you must do them in his way. Ofttimes he would have you ignore temptations instead of fighting them. It is well ofttimes not even to ask, "Who is there," when temptations come knocking at your door.

"Put on therefore, as the elect of God, holy and beloved, bowels of mercies, kindness, humbleness of mind, meekness, long-suffering; forbearing one another, and forgiving one another, if any man have a quarrel against any: even as Christ forgave you, so also do ye." Col. 3: 12, 13. Such a life is a heavenly life. Think these words over and make them your experience today. Have bowels of mercies - that yearning, longing, compassionate feeling that would gladly bring every offender to Jesus for forgiveness. Be kind. Oh, the power of kindness! It can not be resisted; it conquers wherever it goes. This cold world knows no music so sweet as kindness; it charms and delights the ears of all. If you would be kind in word and act, be kind in thought. Be humble in mind. Think well of others and not so well of yourself. Life will flow on peacefully and easily if we are humble; nothing can disturb. Be meek, sweet, and mild tempered. Bear long with the failings and weaknesses of others, carefully considering your own and keeping in mind how you would like to have others bear with you.

"And above all these things put on charity; which is the bond of perfectness." Col. 3:14. Throw the mantle of love over every act and thought in life. Love purely, love sincerely, love fervently. Nothing is so great as love. All the graces have their seat in love; you can not be compassionate, kind, humble, meek, or forbearing without love.

"And let the peace of God rule in your hearts." Col. 4: 15. Let the peace of God act as umpire, deciding every case. Let it have the ruling power in your heart and life today and every day. Whatever matters may arise, let the peace of God take it in hand and dispose of it. If it shows any resistance, then let the peace of God cast it out.

"Let your speech be alway with grace, seasoned with salt, that ye may know how ye ought to answer every man." Col. 4: 6. "Let no corrupt communication proceed out of your mouth, but that which is good to the use of edifying, that it may minister grace unto the hearers." Eph. 4: 29. Have a pure speech, made mighty by the grace of God. Be sober without gloom, be serious with cheerfulness. Have such a conversation as is suited to lift hearts to a higher plane. Your words should be such as to make better those you talk with and make them feel that there is something higher for them.

"Redeeming the time, because the days are evil." Eph. 5:16. Time is more than money; it is life. Do not waste it. Improve its golden moments today. Be economical in its use. Many complain of not having time for devotional reading and for prayer, while if they would examine carefully, they would find that they trifle away as much time as would he needed for prayer each day.

"Submitting yourselves one to another in the fear of God." Eph. 5:21. This is beautiful. Submissiveness is a desirable grace and one that will strew your pathway with peace. How blessed it is to be always ready to give up our way! It is the easy way. We shall find life's way a hard road to travel if we are always wanting our way.

"Be careful for nothing." Phil. 4:6. "Casting all your care upon him; for he careth for you." 1 Pet. 5: 7. "Take no thought for your life, what ye shall eat or what ye shall drink; nor yet for your body, what ye shall put on." Matt. 6:25. The Christian life is one of freedom from anxiety. Jesus will bear all our burdens, and cares if we will but cast them on him. There is no need to worry nor to bear a load of care. A certain brother was much troubled about not having bread for the next meal. But while he was troubling himself and bearing his load, a man drove up and unloaded a barrel of flour at the door. All the time the brother was troubled, the barrel of flour was on the way. Take no anxiety for future things.

"Commune with your own heart upon your bed, and be still." Psa. 4:4. Each evening in some quiet place and with interior stillness talk with your heart and let your heart talk to you. Take a distinctive view of your inward life. You need to be very careful lest you outwardly appear to be a little more than you really are inwardly.

"I am crucified with Christ: nevertheless I live; yet not I, but Christ liveth in me." Gal. 2:20. Is it true? Does Jesus live in you? If you are smitten upon the right cheek, does Jesus then live in you? If you are evil spoken of, misrepresented, misunderstood, neglected, dispised and forsaken, does Jesus live in you then? If you see your brother in need; if you have two coats and he has none, does Jesus live in you then? There are some in prison near you; there are those who are sick; there are those who are thirsty and hungry; in foreign lands there are heathen that know not God, - are you sure Jesus lives in you?

"Behold, I go forward, but he is not there; and backward, but I can not perceive him: on the left hand, where he doth work, but I can not behold him: he hideth himself on the right hand, that I can not see him." Job 23:8,9. This may be your experience some days. In fact, if you are making progress and at all approaching maturity, you will have such experiences. Some dear conscientious Christians become much troubled because they are not more conscious of God's presence. They do not feel him, and thus they conclude they must be very formal. I have always believed and taught that we should have a consciousness of God's presence with us; I still believe and teach it; but I must admit that the most spiritual ofttimes can not perceive God on either hand. They may fear that they are lifeless, because there is not a fresh and sweet spontaneous feeling in their souls. It seems to them that they merely go through the form of worshiping God instead of being in the Spirit. They pray, but their prayers seem to have no depth of heart. In consequence they may be troubled. They need not be. We are not necessarily lukewarm because we do not feel God. The most humble men are those who are least conscious of their humility. The greatest of men are those who take no note of their greatness. The Christian has life; but when we get in the habit of living, we are not so conscious of life.

Let me illustrate the point in this way: Suppose your weakness to be selfishness. You struggle hard against that selfish principle; you notice that you are becoming more unselfish; you are conscious of it because you have had to put forth such effort to attain it; but after you have gained the victory and have become habituated to living an unselfish life, you will be less conscious of your unselfishness. The musician is not so conscious of his skill after he has mastered the art as he is while learning it. Those who are the meekest and have the most intimate converse with heaven, diffusing a fragrance round about them from their holy lives and seeming to be visitants from some world where there is no sin - these are least conscious of their high spiritual attainments.

Live a holy life, obey the commandments of God, have a will to serve God, and if sometimes you do not feel him nor perceive him, do not be troubled, but consider that he knows the way you take and that when he has tried you, you shall come forth as gold.

"Be kindly affectioned one to another with brotherly love." Rom. 12:10. Brotherly love is precious in the sight of angels. It is the most convincing proof of the

Christian religion. "By this shall all men know that ye are my disciples, if ye have love one for another." But in addition to brotherly love there should be kind affection. This is love felt and expressed. There are those who really love, yet whose nature is such that they do not feel much love. Kind affection, like every other grace, is capable of cultivation.

"In honor preferring one another; not slothful in business; fervent in spirit, serving the Lord; rejoicing in hope; patient in tribulation; continuing instant in prayer." Rom. 12:10-12. These words contain depth of experience, but only by prayer and deep meditation can we descend to their depth.

But we must close by referring you to the whole of the Bible. It is a holy book, yea, the holiest of books. A life in harmony with its precepts is the holiest life. Such a life will grace the earth and shine as a star forever in heaven. Cleave to the Bible, study its pages, appropriate its truths to your own heart by faith. By living upon the Word of God, we become more like God. Heavenly words taken into the heart form a heavenly life.

Let your soul be fed each day from the blessed Book of God. Take the time. Drink deep into its pure, crystal stream, and the beauty of the Lord will grow upon you. Watch the little things in every-day life - the thought, the word, the act - until you bring the whole of your life into the habit of acting godly. Be as kind as you can be today, and you can be kinder tomorrow. This is for the Christian. We do not become Christians by growth, but we must grow after we become Christians. We can be more patient tomorrow by being as patient as we can be today. We can be better men tomorrow by being our best today. We grow as we live. If we live the right way, we shall grow that way, and the longer we grow that way, the more natural and easy the way.

Therefore let your whole life flow out in a trend with the Bible, until it wears a channel in holiness and Christian character. Gather food daily for your soul from the sacred page; live in the most intimate communion with God that is possible; meditate in his law day and night; let the love of your heart grow warmer; let life be the holiest possible. Do this, and you will be one of the jewels God will gather to bedeck the temple of the skies.

> A tender blue is in the sky
>   As sets the golden sun;
> Another day is passing by,
>   And thus the moments run;
>
> The song-bird's note is soft and low,
>   Flying to leafy nest;
> In evening's peaceful twilight glow
>   All nature sinks to rest;
>
> The fields are wrapped in somber shroud
>   As fades the light of day;
> A tender flush is on the cloud
>   Beside the milky way;
>
> A hush is on this world of ours;
>   Day, dying, drops a tear;
> Angels' hands unveil the stars,
>   Which one by one appear;
>
> Now Pleiades grow sparkling bright
>   In deepening blue above:

O mild, serene autumnal night!
 Thy voice is full of love.

Such sacred awe my soul doth fill!
 Such quietness doth reign!
The Voice that uttered, "Peace, be still,"
 Has whispered once again.

The silver bars that streak the West
 Are short'ning one by one;
Another day has gone to rest,
 And thus the moments run.

I've one day less to watch and wait,
 My Savior's face to see,
Some day, and ope will be the gate.
 Sweet heaven, I come to thee.

Oh, may it be when sets the sun
 So peacefully and calm!
Oh, may I hear the sweet, "Well done,"
 When evening sings her psalm!

* * * * * * *

It is a pleasant autumn eve;
 The blue is in the sky;
My task is done; I take my leave.
 Good-by, dear friend, good-by!

* * * * * * *

Dear reader, live alone for God;
Walk blameless in his blessed Word.
We may not meet each other here,
But let us live in Heaven's fear,

So when our work on earth is done,
We'll meet each other round God's throne.
Just one request I make of thee:
Until we meet, pray oft for me.

www.ingramcontent.com/pod-product-compliance
Lightning Source LLC
Chambersburg PA
CBHW022359040426
42450CB00005B/249